PILKINGTON

AN AGE OF GLASS

In the mid-1820s a small window glass business was started in the coalfield town of St Helens, near Liverpool, by Richard and William Pilkington – two brothers previously untried in the craft of glassmaking. Within only 50 years, Pilkington Brothers had emerged as Britain's leading manufacturer of flat glass.

An Age of Glass follows Pilkington's growth over 165 years, focusing in particular on the company's development since the Second World War, after which it pioneered the revolutionary float process – the most significant invention in the history of glassmaking.

From its origins as a 19th-century family business, Pilkington has become an international leader in the glass industry. It has constantly outstripped competitors, consistently combining progressive methods of production and the ability to attract skilled glassmakers with shrewd business sense and long-term strategic management. Pilkington's rise to world prominence is a remarkable story of expansion, innovation and success.

T C Barker

TC Barker, previously the first Professor of Economic History at the University of Kent at Canterbury, and now Professor Emeritus of Economic History at the University of London, grew up in St Helens and went to Cowley School there. His graduate research studying the growth of St Helens led to co-authorship of *A Merseyside Town in the Industrial Revolution, 1750–1900* with JR Harris, a contemporary at Cowley and now Professor Emeritus of Economic History at the University of Birmingham. Published in 1954, this was one of the first urban histories to concentrate upon industrial, as well as upon social and local government, developments. His association with St Helens has been maintained by regular visits to work on the extensive Pilkington archives for two previous Pilkington volumes and for the present shorter, updated history of the company.

Professor Barker has also written on transport history, including London Transport, his latest book (written with Dorian Gerhold) being *The Rise and Rise of Road Transport, 1700–1900* (Macmillan, 1993). He is now becoming known to a wider public both as President of the International Historical Congress and by his BBC sound archive programmes on Radio 4.

PILKINGTON

AN AGE OF GLASS

T C Barker

BⓈXTREE

First published in Great Britain in 1994 by Boxtree Limited

This paperback edition published 1994

Text © T C Barker 1994
Photographs © Pilkington plc 1994
(with the exception of page 22, reproduced by permission of
Manchester Public Libraries: Local Studies Unit.)

1 3 5 7 9 10 8 6 4 2

Design and computer make up by Penny and Tony Mills

Printed and bound in Great Britain by Butler & Tanner, Frome, Somerset
for
Boxtree Limited
Broadwall House
21 Broadwall
London SE1 9PL

A CIP Catalogue entry for this book is available from the British Library.

ISBN 1 85283 465 X

JACKET PHOTOGRAPH COURTESY OF PILKINGTON PLC:
*shows a three-dimensional image of the upper layer of a high performance coating on glass.
The image, in which the coating is magnified 200,000 times, was created at the Pilkington
Technology Centre, Lathom, Lancashire,
using atomic force microscopy.*

Contents

Foreword

In 1977 *The Glassmakers* was published. This work of more than 500 pages written by Professor Theo Barker, traced the history of Pilkington from its foundation in 1826 to 1976.

An Age Of Glass, as well as being fully illustrated, brings the Pilkington story up to date and provides an excellent précis of the earlier years of the company described in *The Glassmakers*.

Throughout its history, Pilkington has been notable for inventing and adopting new technology and for being receptive to new ideas and to change. Such attributes have been much needed in the past few years.

The last decade has been as turbulent as any of the fifteen decades which have gone before. Major changes in the composition of the company have taken place against a background of two recessions separated by four years of rapid growth during the late 1980s, a period which also included a successful defence against a hostile takeover bid.

The events of recent years and Pilkington's response to them are well chronicled here. It has been Pilkington's ability to innovate which has enabled the company to play a leading role in the world's glass industry and, by developing the unique properties of glass, to make an important contribution to the quality of life.

Sir Antony Pilkington,
St Helens, November 1993

Introduction: The Story in Outline

A short account of Pilkington's growth over more than 165 years is given chronologically in the following three parts. This summary introduces the reader to the history as a whole and, in particular, brings out the remarkable growth and changes which have occurred since the Second World War.

The window glass business that was started in the mid-1820s at St Helens – then a small but rapidly growing coalfield town of about 5,000 people – by two recently arrived glassmakers and four local residents, emerged within thirty years as one of the three major British window glass producers. A remarkably strong building boom – and a recent halving of the window tax – had encouraged the original founders to venture into the window glass business. Having survived a difficult start by good fortune, the newcomer established itself, in the 1830s, by good management. Helped through difficult years by a family banking connection and its ability to attract to St Helens more skilled glassmakers from elsewhere, Pilkington Brothers was quicker than older rivals to switch to a new method of making window glass, a process that enabled it, a few years later, to take full advantage of the removal of the taxes on glass and windows. In the early 1850s, the company diversified from sheet glass into rough (or rolled) plate glass, a cheaper product, translucent but not transparent, which was in increasing demand for railway station roofs. Subsequently, in the mid-1870s it took a much more momentous decision: to venture, at a newly built factory in another part of the town, into polished plate glass, a luxury product made by casting, not by blowing. This much more costly process produced thicker glass of larger area which had to be ground and polished at considerable expense. The result was completely parallel, distortion-free surfaces that fetched far higher prices, and could be silvered to make mirrors, much in demand for the large, new public houses of the day, or sold to customers who required larger panes, especially for shop windows.

By the 1870s Pilkington Brothers, which had grown in value fifteen-fold in less than fifty years, had become Britain's leading manufacturer of flat glass. The firm increased this lead by adopting tanks in place of pots, which made possible much more efficient round-the-clock melting of sheet and rolled plate, though not yet of polished plate, glass. Strict management and low manufacturing costs, taking advantage of cheap local coal and sand from the firm's own collieries and sandfields, enabled the St Helens business to compete with the greatly increased flow into free-trade Britain of foreign glass imports, especially from Belgium whose glass concerns enjoyed not only low labour costs and weekend working but also cheap transport by water into London – Britain's main market and distribution centre. This competition proved too great for Hartley of Sunderland: it ceased trading in the mid-1890s.

The other British survivor in sheet and rolled plate glass, Chance Brothers of Spon

Lane, Smethwick, continued to exist mainly because it had developed a new means of making rolled plate glass in the 1890s. When patterns were added to the rollers, this cheaper product sold in increasing quantities for windows for the bathrooms that were then being put into more houses; but Chance had failed to make polished plate glass profitably and it lagged far behind Pilkington in the manufacture of sheet. Chance, however, if not so successful in making money out of the main types of flat glass, had always been more science-based than Pilkington. It had concentrated much more upon the optical qualities of glass and especially in lighthouse work; and in the 1930s it ventured into glass fibres. In 1936, at Chance's initiative, Pilkington acquired a 25 per cent stake in the Smethwick business and agreed to acquire the remaining shares in instalments. Majority control was achieved in 1945.

By 1939 Pilkington was virtually the sole British producer of flat glass, though it had to battle hard with importers to retain half the British market in sheet and two-thirds of that in polished (though not in rolled) plate. Its far better performance in polished plate was due to technological leadership. Previously it had adopted the inventions of others; but from the 1920s onwards, it had begun to lead the world with inventions of its own.

In sheet glass, however, it lagged technically behind its international competitors and at one time, in the later 1920s, was on the point of abandoning what was becoming a loss-making mill-stone. The profits from polished and rolled plate glass, however, kept the whole business self-supporting and a new and improved American method for the continuous, flat drawn manufacture of sheet glass became available, just in the nick of time. Pilkington was able to acquire

this Pittsburgh Plate Glass (PPG) process under licence and to develop it further at St Helens during the 1930s; and with the agreed takeover of Chance came not only strength in rolled plate but also knowledge of optical glass and a factory in Glasgow that made glass fibres. Pilkington had also joined forces with Triplex in 1929 to form Triplex (Northern) Ltd to put up a safety glass factory just outside St Helens and, during the 1930s, others overseas. It thus acquired a stake in the processing of glass in the growing new market of the motor industry as well as the supply of raw glass to it.

Three generations of the Pilkington family had done well to bring the business to such pre-eminence by 1939; but it was a pre-eminence that was recognized neither generally in Britain nor abroad. Although Pilkington Brothers, the partnership, had become Pilkington Brothers Ltd, in 1894, with a nominal share value of £1.4 million, it was not yet known to the Stock Exchange because all the shares, apart from a few subsequently disposed of by special arrangement to some of the senior managers, were held by the family either in their own names or in various family trusts. The Pilkington business, therefore, was not discussed in the financial columns of the press. The glass it sold did not carry the Pilkington name either – it was sold anonymously to glass merchants or the motor industry. As the company advertised its wares only rarely, it had no advertising or PR department of its own. Work of this sort was undertaken by one man, John Gloag, a well-known author and member of the London PR firm, Pritchard, Wood and Partners. The Pilkington headquarters remained at St Helens, in or near which those family members involved in its management continued to live. It was still a smoky industrial town where loud factory hooters signalled the beginning of each working day. Directors preferred to travel to meetings elsewhere rather than to bring important visitors to what was called not the head office but 'the works'.

The company did not have a real presence in London until 1950 when it acquired the use of Selwyn House, its imposing but characteristically unostentatious London headquarters tucked away in a cul-de-sac round the corner from St James's Palace facing Green Park. London meetings had previously been held in private rooms at hotels or at British Vitrolite's offices in Albemarle Street. In 1938 it had taken a lease of accommodation on the third floor of Westminster Bank Chambers – the company's bankers – at 63/65 Piccadilly.

Glassmaking still retained its secrets as a craft learned on the job and the prying eyes of outsiders were not welcomed. Pilkington may have become an important national industrial asset by 1939 but this was not generally realized: Pilkington was certainly not a household word outside St Helens as was, say, ICI, Austin or Morris. The main glassmaking concerns elsewhere in the world, a rather gentlemanly group, recognized its existence; but the other members of this exclusive league – and especially the French St Gobain – regarded with some disdain this offshore producer which made all its glass in Britain itself, almost all of it in one place. A second small plate glass factory built near Doncaster during the boom after the First World War had been a costly mistake; and a small plate glass concern at Maubeuge, acquired in the 1890s to give Pilkington a presence within the French ring fence, served to emphasize British inferiority in European terms. In any case, it was closed in 1935.

Pilkington played a much more prominent role after 1945 and gained national recognition even before 1970,

when it became a public company. This was partly because Sir Harry (later Lord) Pilkington, company chairman from 1949 and President of the Federation of British Industries in the early 1950s, remained in the public eye as one of the great and the good who were much sought after to sit on government committees and to chair important royal commissions.

The announcement, in 1959, of a revolutionary new method of making flat glass – the float process, which was to replace sheet and plate glassmaking throughout the world – drew much more attention to Pilkington's national importance as a business; but even before float was fully launched, it was clear that the company was flourishing, as well as innovating, as never before.

Imports of glass into Britain were down to about 10 per cent and exports soared. Whereas in 1934–38 imports of flat glass of all sorts had been two and a half times the sterling value of exports, in 1956–1965 the situation was reversed: exports were three and a half times the value of imports. The tradition that management drive in family concerns declines with the generations was certainly confounded in the Pilkington case. The fourth generation, of which Harry Pilkington was the most prominent member, succeeded as none of the earlier ones had done.

Nor is the turnround in the balance of trade in flat glass the whole story, for Pilkington started to make sheet and rolled plate glass abroad. It had previously confined itself, during the 1930s, to putting down safety glass plants in the Commonwealth to toughen or laminate its UK-made product. Now, having taken the lead on behalf of a consortium of European manufacturers in building a factory in Argentina, which started to make glass at the end of 1938, it began window glass factories of its own in South Africa and

Canada in 1951 and (with local interests) in India in 1954. It gained a greater share in Australian window glass production when the PPG process was installed there at the beginning of the 1960s. Other glassmaking factories followed elsewhere and many additional safety glass plants were put down abroad in the years after the war.

These later developments were made possible largely by the additional strength given to the company by its invention and development of float glass during the 1950s and early 1960s. Whatever technical ascendancy Pilkington may have gained between the wars from its developments in plate glass manufacture was put in the shade by what was, arguably, the most significant invention in the whole history of flat glass. This revolutionary method, invented by Alastair Pilkington, was capable of making glass of plate glass quality much more cheaply by avoiding the costly grinding and polishing processes. It so reduced the amount of fixed capital needed for plant and the working capital needed in its operation that all manufacturers of plate glass throughout the world were soon obliged to take out licences from Pilkington.

Licence fees and other income from the float process helped Pilkington not only to finance further glass manufacture of its own abroad, notably Pilkington Floatglas AB in Sweden, but also to acquire interests in, or control of, other important glassmaking concerns. The most important of these were Flachglas AG, the largest German producer, acquired in 1980, and the glassmaking interests of Libbey–Owens–Ford (LOF), second only to PPG in the United States, acquired in 1986 in exchange for a 30 per cent interest in the whole of the LOF business, which had been acquired from Gulf & Western in 1982.

By the later 1980s, Pilkington, with manufacturing interests in all parts of the world, including Scandinavia, Finland, Australia, New Zealand, South Africa, South America and China, was a very different business from what it had been forty years earlier, just after the Second World War. The last thing it had then contemplated was production of even a single square foot of glass outside the United Kingdom if it could possibly help it, for the maximum loading of the continuous-process machines at St Helens was then the key to profit. By the 1980s, far from being looked at disparagingly by some other international glassmaking concerns, Pilkington was recognized as world leader.

This, however, did not prevent these years of expansion, innovation and success from turning into a time of increasing difficulty and anxiety. If there had been great advantages in Pilkington remaining a private family company, there were great risks to be encountered not in 1970 itself when Pilkington went public, for only 10 per cent of its shares were then offered for sale, but quite soon afterwards when most of the capital in the business came to be held by outside shareholders in general and by a few large financial institutions in particular. The family had always realized that, in an industry depending upon two cyclical markets – building and motors – there would inevitably be leaner years with poorer returns on capital, especially if downswings in both cycles happened to coincide. By prudently allocating profit to reserve in good times and forgoing some dividend in leaner ones, the family management had been able to plan for long-term growth. The costly development of float glass, for instance, was undertaken entirely from the company's own resources – and in complete secrecy. From 1970, however, Pilkington started to attract the full blaze of media publicity. Its annual results were then carefully scrutinized as invest-ment managers of insurance companies and other City institutions acquired more and more Pilkington shares. These new shareholders looked to the company to produce results year by year so that they could receive good dividends on their clients' behalf. Such a short-term view was likely to conflict with the long-term strategies of Pilkington management – and the best interests of its shareholders too, in the longer run.

The events of the 1980s and early l990s, when Pilkington had to weather two cyclical downturns and to persuade the City institutions, by then owning over 60 per cent of the company's shares, to hold on to them rather than to sell – especially when BTR mounted a hostile bid in 1986/87 – will be considered in Chapter 10. The bid failed; but it was soon to be followed by the second, and more serious, cyclical downturn in and after the later 1980s which made the generation of profit much more difficult. Pilkington management had to respond to even greater pressure from the company's owners in the City. So long as it was reliant for profitability on the sale of flat glass – and, as we have seen, much more capital had been invested in flat glass, especially in Germany and the United States – there was no alternative to cutting costs and rationalizing assets. As an insurance, there was also the possibility of diversifying into kindred manufactures not so prone to cyclical swings.

With the acquisition of Chance Brothers, with its optical interests, Pilkington had inherited a quite different, non-cyclical market for glass itself. It developed a shadow factory, Umbroc, at St Helens during the war. In the 1950s, while (Sir) Alastair Pilkington was developing the float process, Dr Lawrence Pilkington, Harry's brother, was paying particular interest to the optical side of the business. In 1957 the purpose-built Chance–Pilkington Optical Works was opened on a green field site at St Asaph in North Wales. Operating a new continuous process under licence from the American Corning Glass Company, it soon became the largest producer of unpolished spectacle glass blanks in Europe. The defence side of the business was also expanded ten years later, in 1967, when a second factory was opened at St Asaph, in collaboration with the American Perkin Elmer company, to make advanced electro-optical systems. (Perkin Elmer ceased to have a financial interest in the undertaking in 1973.) From then onwards Pilkington diversified further into optical and ophthalmic glass: the Michael Birch Group, for instance, in 1974; the Scottish concern of Barr & Stroud in 1977; and Sola Holdings, a large Australian business that operated in eight countries and specialized in plastic spectacle lenses. This was followed, in 1985, by part of the Californian Phalo Corporation, manufacturers of fibre optic communications, and the US Syntex Corporation, makers of contact lenses. In 1987 came the largest purchase of all. Pilkington paid £368 million for Revlon's Barnes–Hind business, with interests in the United States and elsewhere, which also made contact and spectacle lenses, and its Coburn Optical Industries, manufacturers of ophthalmic processing equipment. This and other diversification into branches not so affected by the cyclical movements to which flat glass was inevitably tied, reveals not only sound and sustained strategic thinking over many years, but also a clear policy confidently and relentlessly pursued. It was a strategy, however, that allowed the disposal of those parts of the business, including some recent acquisitions, which did not make, or were not likely to make, sufficient contribution to overall profitability.

Decision-making was, from the mid-1960s, devolved to the various divisions, leaving the board at St Helens

Sir Antony Pilkington

The last link with the family business: Sir Antony Pilkington, the fifth generation to be involved in the company's management, became chairman in 1980.

(in due course six full-time executive directors plus four non-executive members with specialist knowledge outside the company) free to deal with strategic and top-level decisions. The process of management devolution reached its logical conclusion when it was decided to move control of of the main operating division – Flat and Safety Glass (Europe) – from St Helens to Brussels and the large, twelve-storey head office at St Helens, built only about thirty years before, became the subject of a sale and lease agreement. In prospect was a move to more modest

premises a few miles away, with a small headquarters staff. Only 5,300 of the Group's worldwide labour force of 53,800 were left at St Helens in 1992.

Only one family member then remained on the board: Sir Antony Pilkington, knighted for his services to British industry in 1990; but he is Chairman of Pilkington plc. The company, although no longer a paternalistic family concern, still shows particular concern for St Helens, the town upon which its fortunes have been based. Before the government introduced job creation schemes nationally, Pilkington in 1978 took the lead in setting up the Community of St Helens Trust, a local organization giving financial and management help in the creation of new

businesses; and in 1980 it went on to form Business in the Community, this time with national concerns, to identify opportunities that required more capital than would normally be available to a private individual. Further information about these far-sighted initiatives will be found in Chapter 9 and Chapter 10. From the later 1980s, great efforts were made by St Helens itself to attract new businesses to the area and, with the aid of a government city grant of unprecedented sum, to remove the many environmental eyesores left by the coal, chemical and glass industries of the previous century. Derelict industrial sites were thus freed for new housing, business development and amenities of various kinds.

PART ONE

An artist's impression of the St Helens Crown Glassworks, situated on an arm of the St Helens Canal, in the mid-1830s.

To the original crown glass furnace, seen here in the foreground, was added a second, just behind it, in 1834 and a third in 1835. Blown sheet glass manufacture was started at the beginning of the 1840s and the cheaper rough (or rolled) plate glass – translucent but not transparent and in great demand for railway station roofs – towards the end of that decade. The removal of the glass excise duty in 1845 and the window tax, which produced four times the revenue, in 1851, encouraged the more extensive use of glass in building. The three relative newcomers to the industry, Pilkington at St Helens, Chance at Smethwick and Hartley in Sunderland took full advantage of this and became leaders in the British window glass industry at the expense of the older established concerns located in the North East. The number of Pilkington employees grew from 450 in 1849 to 1,350 five years later. None of the three leaders in window glass, however, was yet prepared to venture into the more capital intensive and prestigious cast plate glass branch of the industry. This was represented at St Helens by three other concerns with factories at Ravenhead (the UK pioneer dating from the 1770s), Pocket Nook and Sutton Oak.

1

The First Forty Years:
1826–1869

The St Helens Crown Glass Co. – to give Pilkington its original name – made a very unpromising start and survived its early years as much by good luck as by good management; once established, however, it soon outpaced its older, larger, but less enterprising rivals.

Two of the six original partners, John William Bell and Thomas Bell, who had come to the town a few years before from the main glassmaking centre in the North-East and were already in business as flint glassmakers in a converted factory at Ravenhead, just outside the growing little town of St Helens, were to provide the technical know-how for the new window glassmaking concern, a single-cone works by the Sankey Canal. Of the four other partners, John Barnes, then the only solicitor in the town, was to contribute his legal expertise and James Bromilow, son of the main coal-owner, was to be in charge of the books. Members of two other leading local families were to be called upon for capital alone: Peter Greenall, who had been sent from Warrington in 1818 to take charge of the family brewery in St Helens, and William Pilkington. The initial capital totalled £10,000.

William Pilkington's father had come to the district in about 1780 from the family home in Horwich, near Bolton. He had been

apprenticed to a local doctor and, having walked the wards of St George's Hospital in London, had returned to practise in what promised to grow into a bustling industrial area with a smoky, polluted atmosphere and an increasing number of sickly patients. Alcohol was among all doctors' stock in trade at that time, both for putting the injured or very ill out of some of their pain and as a tonic for those fortunate enough to survive. Most medical men sold wine and spirits on the side and Dr Pilkington was no exception. He built a flourishing business serving the thirsty neighbourhood. So successful was he that, in 1813, while still in his forties, he decided to abandon medicine altogether and a few years later began to rectify spirits as well as to sell them. That is to say, he redistilled plain British spirits bought elsewhere and compounded them with herbs, berries and seeds to add flavour. Two of his sons, Richard and William junior, having served a commercial apprenticeship in Liverpool (William junior to a distiller) joined him and, in 1826, at the age of sixty he himself was able to retire to Windle Hall, which he rented from Sir John Gerard. When he died in 1831, he left a fortune of £20,000. The family was clearly prospering even before it went into glassmaking. By local standards it was well connected, too, for one of Dr Pilkington's

Stock's Farm, Horwich, near Bolton, which Richard Pilkington (1731–1797) leased in 1761, the year of his marriage.

The family fortunes had taken a marked turn for the better two years before when his father, Richard Pilkington senior (1694–1786), successfully claimed a share in land and manorial rights in Allerton, south of Liverpool, after the death without issue of John Hardman, a distant relative by marriage. How Richard Pilkington junior's second son William (1765–1831) came to be apprenticed, in or before his fifteenth year to a doctor in the St Helens area, is not known. It may be supposed, however, that his father knew about the bustling coalmining district to which furnace industries were being attracted because it was on the direct route between Bolton and Liverpool. His father was prosperous enough by that time to afford to send him to London for six months to 'attend the Practice of Surgery' at St George's Hospital from November 1785 to April 1786. He returned to St Helens, and with another aspiring young doctor, took over his former master's practice. The practice flourished amid the increasing number of patients in that increasingly smoke-ridden and polluted atmosphere; but the wine and spirit business, which they, like other doctors, kept, prospered even more. In 1813 Dr Pilkington decided to abandon medicine altogether and, a few years later, began to rectify spirits as well as to sell them.

daughters had married Peter Greenall, taking with her a dowry of £1,000.

In May 1826 when the St Helens Crown Glass Co. was formed and William Pilkington took a two-elevenths share in it, the wine and spirit business was particularly active, for the duties on spirits had just been halved. Soon after February

MANUFACTURE OF HAND-BLOWN CROWN WINDOW GLASS

1. Molten glass, gathered on the end of a blowpipe, was formed into a pear shape by rolling on a marver, a polished iron slab.

2. By reheating, rotating and blowing, a globe was formed.

3. When the globe was of sufficient size, a punty (or solid iron rod) was attached to it opposite the blowing iron which was then cracked off.

4. The globe on the punty was reheated and then rotated at considerable speed so that centrifugal force acting on the edge of the opening caused the metal (molten glass) to be flung outwards, forming a flat disc or 'table'. This operation was known as 'flashing'.

5. The completed table with the bull's eye or bullion in the centre where the punty was attached.

6. The completed tables were piled in a kiln for annealing. The bull's eye, fashionable in some modern front doors, was the least valued part of the crown glass table.

This method of glassmaking survived longer in the United Kingdom than elsewhere because of the way in which the UK glass excise duty was levied, as will be seen when hand-blown sheet glass manufacture is discussed on page 26.

Windle Hall, sketched in 1824.

The wine and spirit business did well and Dr Pilkington became one of the most successful businessmen in the district. In 1821, when his eldest daughter married Peter Greenall, in charge of Greenall's St Helens Brewery, she took with her a marriage dowry of £1,000. Dr Pilkington could afford to retire (aged 61) in 1826. He leased from Sir John Gerard Windle Hall and its surrounding estate for £300 a year. Having fathered 13 children and supported eight of them who survived infancy, he left a personal fortune of £20,000 at the time of his death in 1831. The two sons who went into the St Helens Crown Glass Company in the mid-1820s were already young men of some substance. The elder lived at Windle Hall after his father's death. It was subsequently bought and a member of the family has lived there ever since.

1827, however, when the little glassworks came into production near the banks of the Sankey Canal in what was to be known as Grove Street, J. W. Bell got into trouble with the Excise, being charged with evading tax on glass made at his neighbouring flint glassworks. This soon caused him and Thomas Bell, the only partners who knew about glassmaking, to withdraw altogether from the new window glass venture as it struggled into life. In this emergency William Pilkington, already seen as an astute young businessman though as yet knowing nothing about the glass trade, was called in to take charge. Still in his twenties, he enlisted the help of his brother, Richard, five years his senior. They eventually discovered that Bromilow was not keeping the books properly and Bromilow, together with Barnes, left the firm in 1829. The two Pilkingtons then held eight of the eleven shares, their brother-in-law, Peter Greenall, owning the remaining three. The Pilkingtons remained responsible for the flourishing family wine and spirit business though Richard was able to offload some of its day-to-day management on to their only surviving brother Thomas (born 1804). Peter Greenall's contribution to the glass business was essentially financial.

The Excise authorities, having plunged the new glass firm into difficulties by depriving it of its original managing partners, soon came to its rescue by

An artist's impression of the Chance works at Smethwick, 1857.

Chance Brothers, who established a factory at Spon Lane, Smethwick, near Birmingham, several years before Pilkington, was in its earlier years the more important business. It secured the contract for the Crystal Palace, for instance. James Timmins Chance, who entered the business in 1838 straight from Cambridge where he had read mathematics and had been seventh wrangler in his year, gave the Smethwick firm a considerable technical advantage. It developed optical glass, took on lighthouse work and became market leader in rolled plate. It failed to succeed in cast plate, however, unlike Pilkington which opened its plate glass factory at Cowley Hill, St Helens, in the mid-1870s. Chance was less successful in withstanding the intense competition from continental manufacturers, especially in Belgium, after import duties were removed in 1857. Pilkington emerged as the major British producer, outliving all its older competitors in cast plate glass by 1903 and all its competitors in window glass, apart from Chance, when Hartley ceased production in 1894. Chance continued to do well with rolled plate glass and remained soundly science-based. When Pilkington acquired a 25 per cent stake in the Smethwick business in 1935 and acquired majority control ten years later, it also gained an interest in optical glass and glass fibres.

uncovering a major fraud at its immediate rivals, Mackay, West & Co. Their factory, half-a-mile away near the corner of what were to be called Eccleston Street and Boundary Road, had been in existence for over thirty years. The defalcation caused the partnership to be dissolved and the factory to be put up for sale in 1830. It staggered on under new ownership for a few more years, a shadow of its former self. The resulting switch of customers to the St Helens Crown Glass Co. was an enormous

stroke of luck for William Pilkington as he searched for orders in a period when the building industry was suffering from one of its cyclical downswings.

This luck held. A year or two later Chance at Smethwick ran into difficulties for a spell and, more important, the vast factory at Dumbarton in Scotland, which in its heyday had produced a third as much window glass as all the English factories put together, much of it exported to Ireland, went out of business. In 1834,

Pilkington's nineteenth-century former rectifying plant.

Richard and William Pilkington parted with the profitable family wine and spirit concern in 1837 'from the circumstances of brother Thomas giving up active business and the glass trade growing too heavy for one person to manage'. This photograph, taken in 1971, shows in the foreground the small building which used to serve as the rectifying plant, all the surviving remains of part of what had been Pilkington's earlier business.

Greenall and Pilkington were able to build a second furnace to meet the needs of a strong upswing in the building cycle, and in 1835 a third. These were years of considerable growth and more skilled glassmakers had to be found. Many seem to have been recruited from those thrown out of work when Dumbarton closed.

The extension of the Greenall and Pilkington factory and the increased working capital needed to finance larger stocks of raw materials and finished glass put considerable strain upon the partners' resources. By 1834 they had advanced over £24,000 and there was an overdraft at Parr's Bank in Warrington of just under £10,000. By the end of 1835 this had reached £13,400, and a year later, it exceeded £17,000. Towards the end of 1838, when building demand was slackening again, there are signs that the bank began to grow restive about the size of the firm's overdraft. William Pilkington for a time gave Warrington a wide berth in order to avoid his bankers. On one occasion, in 1838, he told them that he had no time to call and, relating this to his brother, added: 'Any excuse, you will say, is better than none.' In 1840, a sum of £6,000 was raised elsewhere on mortgage; but the bank overdraft nevertheless continued to rise and by 1842 it had reached £20,000. The entire partnership capital then totalled only about £6,000 more than this.

That the bank permitted the overdraft to increase to such an extent at another time of depression, reflects the Greenall influence at Parr's Bank where Peter Greenall's brother, John, was a partner. Without this help, it seems highly unlikely that the additional capital would have been forthcoming to keep the company growing, or perhaps to keep going at all.

It was not until 1836 that William and Richard Pilkington decided that they had to part with the very profitable family wine and spirit business which, William then wrote:

> brought in from 14 to 17 hundred per annum besides keeping our two families... If we could have given up the Glass Works, we should; but from the great outlay of capital in building etc, we should find it next to impossible ... This is a step we at one time never contemplated but from the circumstances of our brother Thomas [aged 32] giving up active business and the glass trade growing too heavy for one person [Richard] to manage to advantage, we thought it much better to give up one than verify the old adage of having too many irons in the fire and letting some burn.

The family wine and spirit business was sold in 1837.

By the early 1840s the growth of the glass business had taken the Pilkingtons into sheet glass. This was made not by spinning the hot glass into a circular disc, as in the crown glass process, but by blowing it into a long cylinder which was then slit longitudinally, opened and flattened out into a large rectangle of glass from which more panes could be cut than from a circular crown glass disc. The firms that took up this more efficient method of manufacture soon gained an advantage over those that did not, especially after the repeal of the duties on glass in 1845, and on windows six years later. The high rate of excise duty, levied by weight of glass melted, had favoured the crown glass process by which the product was (literally) spun out as thinly as possible. Before repeal most of the leading window glass firms had been situated on the Tyne. They failed to switch to sheet, however, and went out of business in the later 1840s and 1850s, leaving most British window glass manufacture in the hands of three firms: Pilkington at St Helens, Chance at Smethwick and Hartley at Sunderland.

Growth at St Helens in the early 1850s had been impressive. The number of Pilkington employees, for instance, increased from under 450 in 1849 to 1,350 in 1854. By the latter date the firm had also acquired the former Mackay, West works. There it made the new and cheaper product, rolled plate glass.

The removal of the glass excise duty and the window tax was accompanied by a steady reduction of the duties on imported glass between 1846 and 1857 when they were completely abolished. This benefited the growing young Belgian glass industry which took advantage of cheap water communication direct to London, the main British market. Retained imports of window glass, almost wholly Belgian, grew from next to nothing in the mid-1840s to 28,000 cwt in 1856, 75,000 cwt in 1860 and 370,000 cwt in 1870, by which time these sales in the British market

MANUFACTURE OF SHEET GLASS

Sheet glass manufacture which Pilkington Brothers embarked upon in the early 1810s, was to their very considerable advantage after the removal of the glass excise duty in 1845. Crown glass had survived only because the excise duty had been levied on the weight of glass melted and this type of glass could be (literally) spun out very thinly. It made smaller panes, however, than could be made by the sheet glass process.

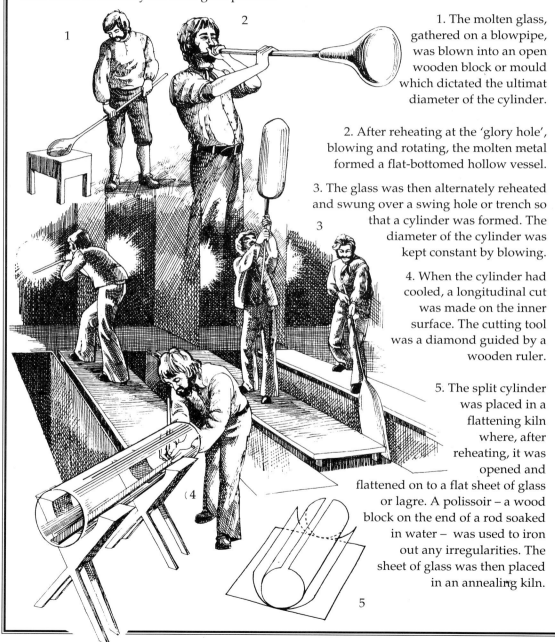

1. The molten glass, gathered on a blowpipe, was blown into an open wooden block or mould which dictated the ultimat diameter of the cylinder.

2. After reheating at the 'glory hole', blowing and rotating, the molten metal formed a flat-bottomed hollow vessel.

3. The glass was then alternately reheated and swung over a swing hole or trench so that a cylinder was formed. The diameter of the cylinder was kept constant by blowing.

4. When the cylinder had cooled, a longitudinal cut was made on the inner surface. The cutting tool was a diamond guided by a wooden ruler.

5. The split cylinder was placed in a flattening kiln where, after reheating, it was opened and flattened on to a flat sheet of glass or lagre. A polissoir – a wood block on the end of a rod soaked in water – was used to iron out any irregularities. The sheet of glass was then placed in an annealing kiln.

EXPANSION OF THE GROVE STREET FACTORY: 1840–1856

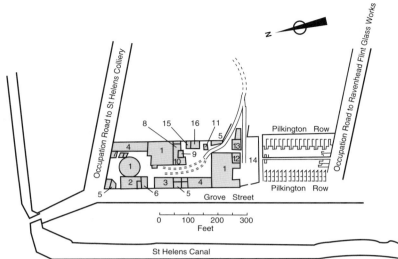

1 Crown Houses
2 Mixing Rooms
3 Warehouses
4 Cutting Rooms with Pot Rooms above
5 Cottages
6 Office
7 Flattening Kilns
8 Engine House
9 Saw Mill
10 Clay Room
11 Brick Kiln
12 Masons Shop
13 Smithy
14 Timber Yard
15 Crate Shop
16 Packing Shop

Greenall and Pilkingtons in 1840

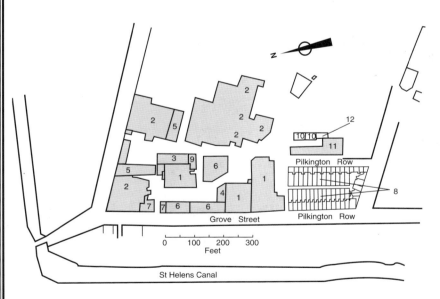

1 Crown Furnace
2 Sheet Melting Furnaces
3 Mixing Rooms
4 Shade Furnace
5 Cutting Room
6 Warehouses
7 Offices
8 Cottages
9 Laboratory
10 Joiners
11 Smithy
12 Experimenting Shed

Pilkington in 1856

Pilkington also owned a rolled plate glass factory nearby which was brought to part of this site in 1872.

William Pilkington (1800–1872)

William Pilkington took a two-elevenths share in the St Helens Crown Glass Company merely as a financial speculation, for he, his brother Richard (who also became financially involved) and another brother, Thomas, were at that time fully occupied with the wine and spirit business. But the four other partners in the glass concern soon withdrew from it. William and Richard found themselves holding eight of the eleven shares and their brother-in-law the other three. Fortunately for the struggling young business, a nearby rival got into difficulties, having been detected in defrauding the Excise, and some of their customers passed to Greenall and Pilkington (as Pilkington came to be known for a time). The Greenall family also had an interest in the Warrington bank of Parr, Lyon and Greenall (subsequently Parr's Bank) and the glass business benefited greatly from unusually generous overdrafts. Greenall was a sleeping partner in the glass business. William Pilkington, the driving force, was the salesman who travelled the kingdom in search of orders. Richard Pilkington was a man of quieter disposition who preferred to stay at home and keep an eye on the office and the works. Peter Greenall, who became MP for Wigan in 1841, withdrew from the glass business in 1842 and died from a stroke in 1845.

almost certainly exceeded those of British manufacturers. In this increasingly competitive situation the British could maintain their output (though not their share of the growing market) only by keeping manufacturing costs as low as possible.

How financially successful was the Pilkington business during its first forty years? This is a question that cannot be answered with any certainty because continuous sets of company accounts go back only to the 1860s. It is clear, however, that during the first half of the period every available pound had to be ploughed back and as much as possible borrowed from the bank and elsewhere. Then, with the rapid growth in sheet glass manufacture, much more capital was needed to finance further expansion and, at some stage, the loans were paid off. Throughout these forty years, that is to say, a very high proportion of the return on capital had to be reinvested. Relatively little was distributed among the partners.

Some indication of this is also to be found in the partners' domestic circumstances. William Pilkington, his wife and their

Richard Greenall

Richard Pilkington (1795–1869)

growing family of fourteen children, the first of whom was born in 1825 and the last in 1849 (twelve survived infancy, six of them boys), lived on the premises of the wine and spirit business in Church Street until they parted with it in 1837. They moved to Millbrook House in Eccleston and then, in 1850, to Eccleston Hall which was leased from its owner, Samuel Taylor, who moved away from the district for a time. (Taylor Park was part of his property before it was presented to the town.) William Pilkington lived at Eccleston Hall until 1869 when, aged sixty-nine, he finally gave up all active interest in

the firm and removed to Downing Hall, near Holywell, where he died a few years later. His elder brother, Richard, who married late and had six children, all boys, lived at Windle Hall which, as we have seen, had been his father's home in his later years. He died in 1869. Neither of the original Pilkington brothers left a particularly large fortune. Richard Pilkington's will was sworn at under £50,000 and William's at less than £100,000.

Only two of each founder's sons were admitted to partnership in the business and to share in its proceeds. The others

had to make their way elsewhere. Three of them, for instance, joined their uncles in the Clifton and Kearsley Colliery near Manchester. Two others became chemical manufacturers at Widnes. Yet another became Town Clerk of St Helens.

For the fortunate four partners of the second generation, however, some very prosperous years indeed were about to dawn, ironically in what has come to be called in the history books the Great Depression.

2

The Second Generation:
1869–1914

The second generation of the Pilkington family – William Pilkington's sons William (Roby) and Thomas, and Richard Pilkington's sons, William Windle and Richard – who took charge of the business during the 1860s, responded with renewed energy to the rapidly growing glass imports. They enlarged, improved and extended the scope of the company's manufacturing operations, embarked upon a vigorous export drive and, eventually, acquired a rival glassworks on the continent of Europe itself. Foreign competition helped Pilkington by driving its weaker British rivals out of business. Left with a straight fight against the continentals, Pilkington's aggressive policy yielded very handsome dividends indeed.

A period of unusually good trade and high glass prices at the beginning of the 1870s provided the capital for the launch into this new and more adventurous phase in the company's history. Net profit reached over 60 per cent on capital in 1872/73. Good profits continued for some time longer. Most of them were ploughed back.

The partners closed down the old and dilapidated works at Cropper's Hill, formerly owned by Mackay, West, and built a new rolled plate factory at Grove Street which began production in 1872. The following year they introduced continuous glass melting by replacing the glassmaking pots, in which the raw materials had to be prepared for twenty-four hours before the molten glass was ready to be worked, by tank furnaces. By feeding in raw materials at one end of a tank, melting them as they passed along and then cooling the molten glass to the correct consistency for working by the time it reached the other end, it was possible to blow glass round-the-clock for the first time. This considerable economy gave Pilkington a decisive advantage over its old adversary, Chance of Smethwick, who clung to the older, intermittent system and ceased to be a serious competitor in sheet glass. Of even greater ultimate importance, however, was Pilkington's decision to build a completely new factory at Cowley Hill, St Helens, for the manufacture of polished plate glass, then particularly sought after and profitable.

The first British factory to make this product on a large scale had been opened at Ravenhead in the 1770s. Two others had been built elsewhere at St Helens, one at Pocket Nook and the other at Sutton Oak, in the mid-1830s. There was also a plate glass factory on the Tyne, on the Thames and in Birmingham; but by the 1860s the three works at St Helens were producing about two-thirds of all British output of

THE PILKINGTON SECOND GENERATION

William (Roby) Pilkington

Thomas Pilkington

William Windle Pilkington

Richard Pilkington

Of the two founders, William Pilkington (married in 1824) fathered 14 children, 12 of whom survived childhood, six of them boys. His elder brother, Richard (married much later, in 1838) fathered six children, all boys. Only two from each side became partners in the glass firm: William's sons William (Roby) (1827–1903) and Thomas (1835–1925); and Richard's sons William (Windle) (1839–1914) and Richard (1841–1908).

The second generation took command of the business when their fathers retired during the 1860s. They brought new initiatives, drive and energy which served the firm well during the more competitive years after 1870. Sales were developed, including those abroad, and manufacturing costs were carefully controlled by technical innovation and a stern labour policy. The company took the very important decision to move into the manufacture of cast plate glass at a new factory at Cowley Hill, St Helens, in the mid-1870s.

this highly priced, quality product. By using its windfall profits of the early 1870s to diversify into this branch of the industry, Pilkington gained a long-term advantage. Chance tried to do so but did not succeed.

The means whereby Cowley Hill should be financed nearly caused a serious rift in the partnership. One branch of the family, William (Roby) and Thomas, wanted to take the opportunity to turn the business into a limited company there and then and to raise some outside capital. (Thomas had six young children to support and his brother ten, some of them of marriageable age.) The other two partners would not contemplate incorporation under any circumstances and, although they had young families, favoured financing the venture out of profits, taking out of the business only a small fixed sum each year. There were some sticky meetings between the parties, including one in London with lawyers present. In the end the reinvestors triumphed over the incorporators. As we shall see, the company was so successful that even the latter must eventually have been very content with the outcome.

Plate glass began to be made at Cowley Hill in 1876 and Windle Pilkington spent much of the rest of his life keeping it right up to date, particularly by the introduction of electrical equipment of all kinds after the 1890s: cranes, grinding benches and so on. Most important among these innovations was the installation in 1904 of a lehr, capable of annealing plate glass continuously, which cut the annealing time from four days to as many hours. Pilkington was gaining technical momentum in its new branch of manufacture, the first important steps along the road to its gaining international supremacy with float glass after the Second World War.

In the early years of Cowley Hill, however, the profits of sheet were required to support plate, for soon after the new factory got into full production, foreign imports of plate glass began to rise even faster than those of sheet, driving prices down and down. Indeed, polished plate glass became cheap enough to provide the impressive windows and mirrors which became so characteristic of the ostentatiously large public houses of later Victorian times. In eight of the eighteen years between 1876/77 and 1893/94, Cowley Hill made manufacturing losses totalling about £141,000; even though in the remaining ten years it returned profits of £281,000 which more than offset these. Nevertheless, the average profit on plate glass over the period as a whole – under £8,000 a year – was insufficient to make its contribution to general overheads and selling costs. Grove Street, on the other hand, was consistently profitable, contributing a net manufacturing profit over the same period of nearly £1,350,000. The other British plate glassworks, which did not have window glass manufacture to sustain them, could not stand the pace and eventually went out of business altogether. Pilkington acquired the old pioneer at Ravenhead in 1901; and when the Sutton Oak works were closed, in 1903, Pilkington emerged as sole British producer of this quality product. This was soon to prove vital to the company's future survival.

By this time international competition in plate glass had become so fierce, and prices had fallen so low, that even the continentals called a truce among themselves. Led by the powerful continental giant, the French-based St Gobain company, an International Plate Glass Convention was formed in 1904 in an attempt to control the European market. Pilkington held aloof at first, though it was prepared to follow the Convention's prices and received notification of changes in these. Meanwhile, it made every effort – with much success –

(RIGHT):An artist's impression of the plate glassworks at Cowley Hill, St Helens, in 1879, three years after its opening.

This was a more heavily capitalized and more fiercely competitive branch of the industry and was only entered into after much debate between the two branches of the family.It survived only because the profits from sheet and rolled plate glass enabled the business as a whole to remain profitable. Pilkington was even able to move into its foreign competitors' territory at the beginning of the 1890s by acquiring shares in a small plate glassworks at Maubeuge, France, close to the Belgian frontier. By 1903 all the other, older cast plate glass concerns in the United Kingdom had failed because of the intensity of Belgian competition. Between the wars, however, it was the turn of Pilkington plate glass to come to the rescue of its sheet; and it was plate, not sheet, which led on to float. In retrospect, therefore, the decision to move into plate glass in the 1870s can be seen as one of the greatest importance.

to improve its plate glassmaking efficiency and to capture a larger share of both home and overseas markets.

For this branch of the glass industry, the Edwardian period saw the real beginnings of international industrial diplomacy, accompanied by threats of price wars and dark mutterings about building rival factories on British soil. In order to strengthen its hand, Pilkington had already had the foresight to acquire on French soil a small plate glass factory

which had been brought to the partners' notice by the works chemist, Douglas Herman, in 1890. It was being built by a French company at Maubeuge, close to the Belgian frontier. Pilkington soon acquired control of it.

Much of the company's success in the later nineteenth century was due to the development of its export trade, particularly in plate glass. The year after Cowley Hill was opened, export sales still totalled only £19,000, £6,000 of which were

in plate glass. Home sales were then worth £312,000. Ten years later, however, in 1887, while home sales had risen to £388,000, exports had shot up to £205,000 (£140,000 in plate glass, £20,000 more than was then sold on the home market).

Pilkington's export trade had, in fact, really begun in 1879 when Richard Pilkington went to America for three months and the firm engaged John Thorpe, who had previously worked for the Wearmouth Company, 'to travel the States and the Colonies'. Unfortunately, there is no record of how this much-travelled

(LEFT): An artist's impression of the sheet and rolled plate glassworks at Grove Street in 1879.

Great economies were made by the introduction of tank furnaces in 1873 which allowed the glassblowers to work round the clock in eight-hour shifts. The smoke from all the chimneys reminds us that Pilkington also owned collieries in the area.

representative covered his extensive territory. He even visited Japan as early as 1882. In 1890 he moved his North American base from New York to Montreal where, two years later, Pilkington opened a warehouse so that glass supplies could be maintained in Canada during the winter when the St Lawrence was frozen. A second warehouse was opened in Toronto in the following year. By 1895 the company had invested £45,000 in Canada. New warehouses were opened in Vancouver (1903), Winnipeg (1906) and Calgary (1912), from which Pilkington travellers covered the whole Dominion. Among them was James Eustace Harrison, eventually to become agent at Vancouver, and then, just before the First World War, Pilkingon's general manager in Canada. He remained the company's proconsul there until 1945, not only dealing with Canadian matters but also gleaning all the intelligence he could about any significant glassmaking developments in the United States and relaying this valuable information without delay to St Helens.

Other Pilkington men, sent out from the United Kingdom, came to represent the company in other parts of the world, notably J. L. Kimmins in the Far East from 1902, Harold Mees in Australia from 1904 to 1932, Frank William Butcher in New Zealand from 1912 to 1929, and Joseph Brooks in South America from 1911 to 1946. In the days before the spread of international air travel and air mail services, all these men felt very far from head office. Confronted with increasing competition yet not given the freedom to cut prices to meet it without permission from St Helens, they often found it difficult to understand the thinking behind the instructions received from there.

In the years between 1874 and 1894 the firm's capital value grew more than nine-fold, from £150,000 to £1,400,000. The business was then turned into a private limited company with £800,000 in ordinary shares and £600,000 in 5 per cent debenture stock. This did not involve admitting non-family shareholders, for there was no need to seek any outside capital. Profits were good enough to sustain further growth. They continued to grow, nearly £3 million being retained in the company between 1894 and 1914. Much of this went into the factories. The value of Cowley Hill was put at nearly £1,200,000 in 1914 and that of Grove Street at over £700,000. The company also had considerable reserves,

including about £350,000 invested outside the business, mainly in a wide selection of foreign securities. By then Pilkington was employing close on 10,000 people.

Despite the high rate of reinvestment and allocation of profit to reserve, business was so good during the forty years between 1874 and 1914 that there was still much profit left for distribution among the family shareholders. During the first half of the period, when £1,250,000 was re-invested, £725,000 was distributed among the four partners. During the second half, from 1894 to 1914, nearly £3,000,000 was reinvested, and about £2,300,000 was distributed to the family shareholders of the new company, who numbered ten at the time of its formation, three of the senior partners each having handed over a few of their shares to two of their sons. The four Pilkingtons of the second generation certainly reaped the financial rewards of their success on a scale far greater than their two fathers had done over roughly the same number of years in the business. Richard Pilkington left £693,000 gross, Windle Pilkington £590,000, Thomas Pilkington £689,000 and William (Roby) Pilkington, who presumably had trans-ferred most of his fortune to his sons before his death, £108,000.

This, however, is not the end of the pre-1914 part of the story. Unusual success, and the sense of well-being that goes with it, sometimes means that rash decisions are easier to make. To some extent this may be attributed to management weaknesses in the third generation, who took over control of the company in the few years leading up to the First World War. Their predecessors had been physically tough, escaped accidents and lived long. In the third generation, however, Thomas Pilkington's eldest son was killed in the Boer War and one of Windle Pilkington's twin sons, Henry, fell ill with lung trouble

(LEFT): Busby Lane warehouse, Canada, c.1913.

Pilkington developed a large export trade in the last quarter of the nineteenth century. Its first warehouse in Canada was opened at Busby Lane, Montreal, in 1892 and a second in Toronto a year later. By 1914 others were operating across Canada, from which Pilkington travellers covered the whole Dominion.

(RIGHT): James Eustace Harrison (1878–1949).

Pilkington representative in Canada from 1912 to 1945, from where he also reported on all glassmaking news from the United States, J.E. Harrison had joined Pilkington in St Helens as a trainee in 1891. After serving very briefly as a traveller operating from its Nottingham depot, he was posted in 1911 as agent in Vancouver and then, in the following year, at Montreal. When Pilkington Brothers (Canada) Ltd was formed in the mid-1920s, J. E. Harrison became a director of that company.

Pilkington's plate glassworks, Cowley Hill, in 1914.

When Pilkington Brothers became a private limited company in 1894, its shares were valued at £1.4 million. Between then and 1914, a further £3 million was ploughed back into the business from its profits. The factories were kept right up to date technically. Cowley Hill was valued at nearly £1.2 million in 1914 and Grove Street at more than £700,000. When the company bought the old pioneer plate glass factory at Ravenhead for £93,000 in 1901, it was found that manufacturing costs per square foot there were well over 50 per cent greater than those at Cowley Hill.

and died in 1902. Other Pilkington sons were available but were not always of their parents' calibre. The company saw fit to bring in a non-Pilkington who had married into the family, and he was to play a notable part in the difficult inter-war years.

3

Between the Wars

The British building industry flourished from the early 1920s as never before, thanks to subsidized council housing, falling interest rates, the spread of building societies and the growth of middle-class home ownership. In consequence house-building was hardly affected, unlike many other industries, by the world depression of the early 1930s. In this respect, unlike the position half a century later, flat glass manufacture was at an advantage. More-over, since houses were now expected to be brighter and airier, more glass was put into each of them. The new motor industry also provided a small but rapidly growing market after 1920. It, too, weathered the depression well and also required more glass per unit. The saloon cars of the 1930s, even the smaller ones which then became popular, required more than just the windscreens that were all the open tourers needed in the early days of motoring. Pilkington should have done well in these circumstances and have excelled its pre-1914 performance; but it did not do so. The weakened third generation, as it gained control in the years just before 1914, had been too impatient to innovate.

Before 1914, the greatest economies in glassmaking had been gained from the transforming of intermittent into continuous processes. As we have seen, the introduction of tank furnaces in the 1870s and 1880s had made melting, the first stage in sheet glassmaking, continuous; but the subsequent blowing and flattening were still done a cylinder at a time. Early in the present century, the American Window Glass Co. developed a machine that would perform the work of lower grade blowers by drawing up from a specially constructed pot of molten glass, a single large cylinder forty feet long. This reduced the cost of blowing, but not of flattening; and the process was still intermittent as cylinders had to be blown by the machine one at a time. In America, where skilled glassblowers' wages were considerably higher than in Europe, this new drawn cylinder process had a particular attraction. When, in 1905, the American Window Glass Co. gave notice that it proposed to put down a drawn cylinder plant in Canada, Pilkington felt obliged to respond. It secured a licence to operate the process in both Canada and Britain. The new machinery began to produce its large glass cylinders at St Helens in 1910 and at a specially built factory at Thorold in Canada a few years later. By 1915 over £220,000 had been invested there but the factory lost money – by 1918 £130,000 had been lost. However, Pilkington was to lose much more before Canadian production finally ceased in 1924.

FLAT GLASS MANUFACTURE

The goal in flat glass manufacture was to move from intermittent to continuous production. This was achieved in sheet glass before it was reached in plate, though for a time Pilkington ran into difficulties by adopting a halfway process in the former. The first step in sheet glass manufacture – melting – had been made continuous by the substitution of tanks for pots from the early 1870s. Some progress was made in the forming of the glass when blowers were able to use compressed air at the end of the nineteenth century. Early in the twentieth century the American Window Glass Co. developed a machine capable of drawing from a specially constructed pot of molten glass a single cylinder 40 feet long. Although this blew more glass at a time, it was still an intermittent process and was incapable of making glass of the highest quality.

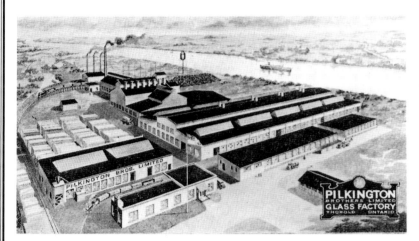

When AWG threatened to operate the process in Canada, Pilkington responded by taking a licence for Canada and for the United Kingdom. Cylinder drawn production started at St Helens in 1910 and, shortly afterwards, at a specially built factory at Thorold on the Welland Canal, south-west of Hamilton, Ontario.

(LEFT): Pilkington's Thorold factory in Ontario, Canada.

Blown Cylinder Manufacture At The Turn Of The Century

(RIGHT): A glassblower using `bicycle' apparatus and compressed air.

Mechanized Cylinder Process At Sheet Works

(RIGHT): Filling a reversible pot by ladle from the tank.

(BOTTOM LEFT): The start of the draw.

(BOTTOM RIGHT): The finished cylinder being lowered on to a cheval prior to being cut and split.

Flat Drawn Sheet Glass (using PPG process)

While Pilkington was committed to drawn cylinder glass, more promising continuous processes were being developed, the sheet of glass being drawn directly from the tank and then passed through the lehr. The two processes, developed by competitors, Libbey-Owens and Fourcault, cut costs to such an extent that, by the later 1920s, Pilkington was on the point of abandoning sheet glass manufacture altogether. Then, in the nick of time, a third flat drawn process became available, developed by the Pittsburgh Plate Glass Co., and superior to the other two. Pilkington began to install it under licence at St Helens at the beginning of the 1930s, eventually signing the licence in 1931.

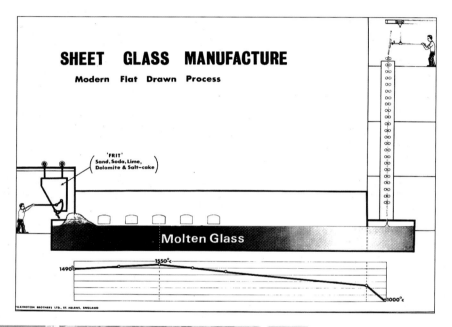

(ABOVE): Diagram of PPG process.

(LEFT): View of the edge of the glass ribbon leaving the tank. Edge rollers can be seen on either side of the glass, towards the bottom.

(OPPOSITE): The glass is cut at the top of the annealing tower and sheets are lifted off.

44

Plate Glass

(LEFT): Early plate process: the men in the centre are lifting the pot of molten glass and pouring it on to the table. Those to the right of them roll the glass into a plate.

(BELOW): `Swimming the plate': laying the plate on a large circular disc for grinding and polishing.

Important developments took place at Cowley Hill between the wars which enabled plate glass to repay the debt it owed to sheet for its survival in the later nineteenth century.

One of the old-fashioned, labour-intensive stages in cast plate glass manufacture before 1914 was 'swimming the plate' prior to its grinding and polishing. The molten glass had still to be produced intermittently in pots to maintain the clearest transparency needed for thicker panes. After 1920, in collaboration with the Ford Motor Co., Detroit, Pilkington developed a method whereby a ribbon of glass was rolled out of a tank. The ribbon was then passed under a series of mechanically-driven grinding and polishing heads. A twin grinder, which dealt with both surfaces simultaneously, was later developed and the company was well on the way to developing a continuous polisher, too, in

(ABOVE): View along the twin grinder at Cowley Hill Works, 1944.

(ABOVE): The ribbon of glass passing between twin grinding heads.

The drawn cylinder machines at St Helens managed to make money but they involved Pilkington in problems that were more far-reaching in their effects than those in Canada. While it was investing in this intermittent plant to manufacture the lower qualities of sheet glass – the better qualities were still blown by hand – two other processes were then being developed which *were* continuous, could in time make the better qualities and did, in fact, replace all the old skilled glassmakers, flatteners as well as blowers. The American Libbey–Owens process and the Belgian Fourcault process, both using different techniques, drew the glass out of the tank in a wide ribbon and passed it through a lehr at the end of which it emerged, annealed and ready to be cut and sent to the warehouse. The drawn cylinder machinery was soon obsolete; but Pilkington, committed to it, delayed too long in its attempts to secure a licence for either of the flat drawn methods. They found themselves as late as the mid-1920s having to install more drawn cylinder machines as a substitute for the more costly handblowers, just to remain in the race with the Libbey–Owens and Fourcault manufacturers, then producing greater proportions of good saleable glass and extending their plant in Europe and elsewhere. In the 1920s, foreign imports from there captured most of the growing British market. Fortunately for Pilkington a third, and superior, flat drawn process, developed by the Pittsburgh Plate Glass Co. (PPG), became available just when St Helens was considering abandoning sheet glass manufacture altogether. It was installed at St Helens during the early 1930s and enabled Pilkington sheet glass to become fully competitive once more.

In plate glass the company suffered no such setback in the 1920s; indeed, plate glass manufacture, having been kept alive by the profits of sheet in the highly competitive years of the later nineteenth century, now, for a time, had to return the compliment. By developing, to some extent in collaboration with the Ford Motor Co. of Detroit, a tank furnace capable of producing, in a continuous flow, the higher-quality melt required for plate glass manufacture and a continuous grinder and polisher (later further developed into a twin grinder which ground both surfaces simultaneously) Pilkington became technically the most advanced plate glassmaker in the world. It had almost managed to turn the whole of plate glass manufacture into a continuous process; only a twin polisher remained to be developed. Yet even in this branch of the business, so go-ahead and so profitable, another premature investment decision by the third generation was to prove particularly costly to the company.

As we have seen, the continental manufacturers had, in 1904, joined together in an International Plate Glass Convention. They threatened on more than one occasion to build a plate glass factory in Britain in order to break Pilkington's monopoly of British production, in much the same way as Pilkington had acquired its own Maubeuge works within their ring fence. Just before the First World War began, Pilkington seems to have reached a decision to put up what was described as an East Coast Works to counter this threat. The company returned to this project as soon as the war was over.

A site was selected at Kirk Sandall, four miles east of Doncaster on a canal that gave direct access to the Humber and the North Sea. The company could not have chosen a worse time for this project. Building costs escalated greatly in the post-war boom and when the new Doncaster factory came into full production at the end of 1922, it had already cost the company nearly £1,900,000. It swallowed up not only many of the vast reserves accumulated before and during the war, but also £1,000,000 in new capital which had to be raised from the family shareholders in 1920. Worse still, very soon after Doncaster began to make plate glass, its plant was rendered obsolete by the new improvements introduced in that particuar form of glassmaking. The board soon had to look around for other products which could be made there and other companies to take up some of the vacant space.

The third generation of Pilkingtons obviously had not managed to maintain their predecessors' impressive record. A contributing factor had been unexpected family losses, as we have seen, and Windle Pilkington's other twin son also suffered from tuberculosis. This was Austin Pilkington who became very seriously ill in 1907 and – in a last desperate attempt to save his life – was sent to live in Colorado, where the air was particularly dry and thin. There he recovered after many months. Richard Pilkington's eldest son, Arthur Richard, who had become chairman of the company in 1914, died in 1921 at the age of fifty; and Thomas Pilkington's remaining son, Alan Douglas, decided to retire, mainly on grounds of ill-health, at about the same time. (He was only forty-one – and lived on to the ripe old age of ninety-four.) All these losses placed greater burdens on the three remaining senior family directors who had to bear the main responsibility for the running of the business: Austin Pilkington, now completely recovered, and chairman from 1921, his younger brother Cecil and their brother-in-law Edward Cozens-Hardy. The latter, who had grown up at the family home, Letheringsett Hall, Holt, in Norfolk, had been a partner in the prestigious London electrical engineering consultants,

O'Gorman and Cozens-Hardy. He joined the Pilkington family at one remove when his sister, Hope, married Austin Pilkington in 1903. He was brought into full-time management in 1908 after his brother-in-law had left to recover from his illness in America and stayed there after his return. The son of an eminent lawyer, later Master of the Rolls, he became the third Baron Cozens-Hardy in 1924.

The company's financial position, which deteriorated between 1925/26 and 1927/28 as increased borrowing (to finance its capital developments in plate glass) was accompanied by diminishing manufact-uring profits, enjoyed a couple of years of recovery as markets improved, but then collapsed in the year ended March 1931, reflecting to some extent the fate of the British economy at that time. Pilkington's manufacturing profits fell from £572,000 to £135,000. A half-yearly dividend had to be passed.

The strain of management became too great for the triumvirate. Matters came to a head at the end of 1931. One day in the lunch room, Austin Pilkington 'had words' with his brother Cecil. (According to Austin's son, Harry Pilkington, Cozens-Hardy seized his opportunity to slip out in order to avoid having to take sides.) Both brothers resigned from active manage-ment, though they still undertook particular duties and continued to sit on the full board. An executive committee was thereupon set up to run the business with Cozens-Hardy as its chairman and R. M. Weeks as his right-hand man. (Weeks had been recruited from Cambridge in 1911 as Pilkington's first management trainee.) To this executive two non-family directors were also added (William Stuart Tunnock and John Herbert Dickinson) and a committee structure, in which senior management became associated, began to be worked out for the administration of the

Three third-generation Pilkingtons and three senior managers visit the site of the future plate glassworks at Kirk Sandall, Doncaster, in 1919. (LEFT TO RIGHT): R. M. Weeks, W. N. Pilkington, R. A. Pilkington, H. Mees (Australia), E. H. Cozens-Hardy, F. E. Slocombe.

The third generation of Pilkington management did not enjoy the same success as those who went before or who came after. To some extent this was because of early death or retirement. One eligible Pilkington was killed in the Boer War and another, who survived it, decided not to return to the company. Richard Austin Pilkington (1871–1951), whose twin brother had died of tuberculosis in 1902, became so ill himself with TB that he was sent for some time after 1907 to Colorado. It was thought that the thinner, healthier air there rather than the heavily polluted atmosphere of St Helens would be more conducive to his recovery. Although there were no losses among the directors in the First World War, one of them decided to retire in 1921, mainly on grounds of ill-health – and went on to live to be 94. Another, Arthur Richard Pilkington (born 1871), who had served as company chairman from 1911, died in 1921. During that difficult decade of the 1920s, Richard Austin Pilkington, fully recovered, became chairman and his younger brother, Alfred Cecil Pilkington (1875–1950), served as senior technical director.

There were two other very important men on the technical side. Edward Herbert Cozens-Hardy (1873–1956) whose sister had married Austin Pilkington, had been recruited to the board in 1908 when it was feared that Austin Pilkington might never return to the business. He was a great asset, for he had been partner in the electrical engineering consultants, O'Gorman and Cozens-Hardy of Victoria Street, London. He encouraged electrification in Pilkington factories, especially at Cowley Hill, and favoured the appointment of a number of electrical engineers who subsequently proved to be outstanding factory managers. His father, a Lord Justice of Appeal and subsequently Master of the Rolls, had been created the first Baron Cozens-Hardy in 1914 and Edward succeeded to the title in 1924 on the death of his elder brother.

Ronald Morce Weeks (1890–1960) joined Pilkington direct from Cambridge in 1912 as a technical trainee, was mentioned three times in despatches during the war and received the DSO, MC and bar. Returning to Pilkington, he was appointed manager at Cowley Hill in 1920, a sub-director in 1921 and a director in 1928. During the Second World War he was to become Deputy Chief of the Imperial General Staff and after it Chairman of Vickers Ltd as well as director of various other companies, serving Pilkington as a non-executive director until his death (in 1960). He was created Baron Weeks of Ryton in 1956.

Harold Mees, photographed here during a spell of home leave, was another of Pilkington's important proconsuls abroad. In 1904, when a clerk in the company's Sheffield warehouse, he had been sent to Australia as its agent, working on commission until 1910 when he joined the salaried staff. He remained Pilkington's agent in Australia until 1932.

F. E. Slocombe, apprenticed as a fitter and turner, joined the company in 1887 and rose to be one of Pilkington's most outstanding factory managers. He became manager of the Doncaster works until he reached retirement age in 1938, after 51 years' service.

A. R. Pilkington (1871–1921)

A. C. Pilkington (1875–1966)

John Dickinson   *Geoffrey Langton Pilkington*   *William Tunnock*

In 1931, when Pilkington had the very unusual experience of passing a half-yearly dividend, Austin and Cecil Pilkington resigned from active management. Lord Cozens-Hardy became chairman of a newly-formed executive committee with Ronald Weeks as his right-hand man. Two non-family members became directors. John Herbert Dickinson (1870–1958), who had joined the company in 1905 to help his father handle the legal business, became director in charge of the legal department. William Stuart Tunnock (1877–1947), son of Pilkington's Scottish agent, who had joined the Glasgow office in 1891 to become a traveller in Scotland and Glasgow agent in 1912–1913, was appointed company secretary at St Helens in 1920. In 1931 he became director in charge of the sales and commercial department. Geoffrey Langton Pilkington (1885–1972), the oldest of the fourth generation of Pilkingtons who had joined the firm in 1909, served in the Royal Flying Corps in the First World War and became a director in 1921. He became chairman of the company from 1932 to 1949 and of its executive committee between 1939 and 1947.

business as a whole. A first tentative step had at last been taken in the long-overdue process of transforming into a well-structured modern business what, despite its creation as a company in 1894, was still in reality a creaking family partnership.

The fourth generation of the family also began to play a greater part in this transformation. Geoffrey Langton Pilkington, William (Roby) Pilkington's grandson, much older than his cousins, had been a director since 1919 and was to serve as chairman of the full board from 1932 until 1949. The others, some of whom had started to work for the company in 1927, had served a much more rigorous probation. Under the Cozens-Hardy regime their period of trial was as searching as it was prolonged, for the managers of the departments or works in which it was being served made regular reports on their progress. This was no mere formality. William Lee Pilkington, for instance, one of those who had started in 1927, was in 1933 offered 'a final trial for a period of one year'. He did not succeed in satisfying his examiners and eventually left the company. But Harry Pilkington, who read History and Economics at Cambridge, and Douglas Phelps, son of a Pilkington daughter, who read Chemistry

James Bonar Watt   *James Meikle*

Under the Cozens-Hardy regime, the selection of Pilkington family members, which included sons of Pilkington daughters as well as sons of Pilkington sons, was made more rigorous than ever. Those who succeeded in clearing the various management hurdles will be considered in due course. They were joined during the 1930s by two other non-family directors. James Bonar Watt, who had been with Pilkington since 1914, had achieved great success in installing and developing the PPG sheet glass process and had become manager of the sheet glassworks in 1936. James Meikle, an electrical engineer by training, had also joined the company in 1914 and risen to be the plate glassworks manager in 1931. Both were Scots, educated at Allan Glen's School, Glasgow. So, too was W. S. Tunnock. One of Pilkington's medical officers, James Rutherford Kerr, son of a headmaster of the school, played an important part in establishing the connection.

there, reached the executive committee in 1934, to be followed by Roger Percival in 1936 (another such son, an Oxford graduate and Olympic hurdler) and Peter Cozens-Hardy, Lord Cozens-Hardy's son, in 1937. By then Lawrence Pilkington, who had read Natural Sciences at Cambridge, and Arthur Cope Pilkington, ex-Coldstream Guards, had also begun to go through the usual hoops and over the usual hurdles and were to join the executive committee in the 1940s. There was another important recruit to it from the ranks. This was James Meikle, an electrical engineer by training, who joined the executive in 1936.

The new regime placed more emphasis on budgetary control. Cozens-Hardy took charge of this and gave P. L. Robson, the company's one and only chartered accountant in 1931, three younger colleagues to assist him. One of them, J. B. Bowden, was to become his deputy and ultimately his successor (1961–68). The National Institute of Industrial Psychology was called in to conduct a six-month study of the recruitment, selection and training of clerical staff; and time study was introduced at the works. A personnel department was formed and a management trainee scheme started. Central Research Laboratories were built to which

scientists were brought in from the works or specially recruited from outside. A new, oval-shaped head office, built out from the existing one at the entrance to Sheet Works, symbolized the progressive changes of the 1930s – and accommodated the additional staff that those changes had necessitated.

During the 1930s the company strengthened its manufacturing position by the successful installation and improvement of the PPG flat drawn sheet glass process – for which chief credit must go to J. B. Watt – and the introduction of the twin grinder at Cowley Hill, the culmination of developments there for which F. B. Waldron was mainly responsible. It also took over a factory at Queenborough in Kent, after a competitor's attempt to work the Fourcault process there. With the takeover of its long-established rival, Chance Brothers, Pilkington also acquired a stake in optical glass and glass fibres. As part of the government's special area policy, it also

found itself obliged to start window glass manufacture at Pontypool in 1938.

Pilkington took advantage of the rapidly growing motor industry by supplying raw glass to the safety glassmakers and by acquiring a majority interest in Triplex (Northern) Ltd whose factory in Eccleston came into production in 1930. This development soon gave rise to Pilkington safety glass plants abroad, notably in Australia where a very successful subsidiary company began production in 1935 and caused Pilkington to become involved with the Australian Window Glass Co., then struggling to produce sheet glass of a rather inferior quality behind a tariff wall.

Pilkington's trading results improved again as the world economy emerged from the depression and the company's new administrative arrangements – and new directors – proved their worth. The crisis was past and the foundations had been laid for a future that was brighter than ever.

4

The Changing Face of Management

Pilkington was providing recreational facilities and part-time schooling for its employees by the middle of the nineteenth century. Medical services were introduced in the 1880s, and superannuation and pensions schemes after the First World War. Holidays with pay and children's allowances followed in the later 1930s. The firm was not a pioneer in any of these developments – both Cadbury and Rowntree had brought in contributory pensions for their wage earners by 1906, for instance – but it was ahead of many other major companies such as ICI, which provided pensions only after 1937, and Courtauld. Most important, Pilkington was still able to provide work when other local concerns went out of business. A job with Pilks was much sought after. Sons – and, later, daughters – followed their fathers into the business.

Pilkington's recreation section dates from 1847. Cricket appears to have been the main interest of members at the outset; but by the early 1860s there was a bowling green and a skittle alley attached to the cricket field, near present-day Kirkland Street. A building was put up there where members could play billiards, draughts and other games. When the Cowley Hill factory was opened in the 1870s, a second sports ground was opened nearby. The

rugby section was formed in 1879 and in 1884 the 'Recs' joined the West Lancashire and Border Town Rugby Union. The present recreation ground in Ruskin Drive dates from 1901. In 1938 it was allowed a bar, but with some misgivings and only after the full Pilkington board had discussed the matter.

From about 1850 the company ran a free school for boys in their employment who were expected to attend classes for an hour or two either in their own time after work or by arrangement with managers and foremen during the daytime. Classes grew in size and by the end of the century the schoolmaster had two assistants. Pilkington's school was taken over by the St Helens Local Education Authority early in the present century.

The firm's medical services date from 1882. Although there had previously been arrangements between Pilkington and various doctors in the town for medical attention in case of accidents at the works, the employees had been obliged to rely on one or other of the town's numerous friendly societies for assistance in case of illness. Towards the end of 1881, the skilled glassblowers, who already ran such a sickness and burial society among themselves, asked if they might hold meetings at the works instead of at a public

house. Pilkington agreed but asked them to consider extending their club to all the other employees at Grove Street. Within a short time the firm was negotiating with local doctors to attend nearly 1,200 employees and their wives and daughters. Local doctors continued to be employed until 1905 when the club appointed a doctor of its own. Meanwhile, there had been complaints of club members feigning illness, which caused the board to make the characteristic comment in its minutes: 'Much more sickness now than before the Club existed. No doubt some rascality exists.'

The Pilkington directors of the second generation who made that remark were renowned for their sternness. Soon after they took over control, in the later 1860s, they launched a great economy campaign. Some men were laid off and others demoted. At least one of them refused the

(LEFT): The office at Grove Street in the mid-1920s.

Pilkington's business had grown to such an extent that a new general office was opened at Grove Street in 1887, just outside the entrance to the Sheet Glassworks. The building was designed by J. Medland and Henry Taylor, Manchester architects who specialized in churches. The family directors, too, were hard at work in individual offices immediately off this vast hall where they could be seen at their desks through a circular window in each door. They were also glimpsed by the rest of the office staff as they entered and left. Women came to be employed in the years immediately before 1914.

new terms which were offered. The board minutes record what happened:

> Told T. Glover that we had decided to put him to the trowel again when he at once replied that he had been expecting it as the work and reduced staff wouldn't warrant his remaining in his present position: but though he should be willing at any time to have the trowel to work *piece work* for us, he should decline to take it otherwise. This, of course, settled the matter and he goes.

This severe attitude was to provoke the most protracted strike in Pilkington's history, far longer than the much publicized seven-week unofficial stoppage in 1970. The sheet glassblowers stopped work in April 1870, and the other glassmakers had to be laid off. The firm maintained a token output for over six months using younger managers and apprentices. When the strike eventually ended, on 5 November, the men came back on their masters' terms.

A trade union, the Sheet Glassmakers' Association, formed at this time, survived the strike and called another one in 1878 when, because of a fall-off in trade, wages were again being cut. This was only a partial stoppage, however, for a number of workmen refused to support it. It began on 9 August but had petered out by mid-November, the men again returning on their masters' terms. As they came in, they were obliged to sign six-month contracts, arranged so that each expired at a different date, which meant that only a small section could, in future, strike at any one time without breaking their agreements. Lower rates of pay were introduced, but when the *non*-strikers came to be bound by these new rates, they were granted a bonus of £5 per year, subject to their being 'steady and sober' and behaving to the firm's

satisfaction. This put an end to strikes at Grove Street. Nor is anything more heard about the Sheet Glassmakers' Association.

Other attempts were made to form trade unions, but the company refused to recognize any of them. When, however, in 1906, over 500 blowers and gatherers (out of a possible total of perhaps 750) were said to belong to a union and the flatteners were also reported to be strongly organized, the directors did speak to mass meetings and received formal deputations from their own men. The minutes suggest that some of these meetings may have provided real opportunities for the airing of genuine grievances and, moreover, that these were looked into. Yet on pay and union recognition the company refused to yield to pressure. When in 1911, for instance, a Pilkington employee asked about a letter sent to the company by Tom Williamson, the union organizer, he was told that such a letter was not from a workman and it had been thrown into the fire.

Union recognition eventually came in 1917 as part of a new national climate influencing industrial relations. Having recognized the National Amalgamated Union of Labour (from 1924 part of the National Union of General and Municipal Workers) – the union Tom Williamson represented – the next generation of Pilkington directors got on well with it and there was only one small strike throughout the inter-war years, of glasscutters at Doncaster at the end of the 1920s. Pilkington's glassworkers were not involved at all in the nine-day General Strike of May 1926 and the NUGMW's District Secretary even promised, if need be, to use his influence with the railway unions to ensure that coal got through to keep the glassworks going at St Helens. Pilkington's Joint Industrial Council, set up in 1919, became an important forum of discussion, enabling management and labour to grapple together with the company's inter-war problems. These included redundancies arising from the transition from skilled glass blowing to machine production, alleviated to a considerable extent by a special glass-makers' compensation fund into which Austin and Cecil Pilkington paid £28,000 from their own pockets between 1927 and 1933.

Tom Williamson, whose letter had been so unceremoniously burned in 1911, became the union's able and under-standing negotiator after 1917. In 1938 when he was about to retire and the directors heard that he was likely to be in straitened circumstances, they consulted the union's general secretary to see whether it would be in order to subscribe to the collection being made by his fellow trade unionists. The company not only made a contribution but also bought him a small annuity.

As the business grew, the Pilkington family came to depend increasingly on executives promoted to senior positions. One of the first of them was John J. Wenham, recruited in 1868 from Richard Evans & Co. to take charge of the rolled plate department. He was then earning £2 a week but, as he took over more responsibility, his salary was steadily advanced until, by the mid-1880s, it reached the very considerable figure of £1,000 a year. (An unskilled wage was then under £1 a week or less.)

It was for their technical specialists that Pilkington came to depend mainly on outside recruitment. Henry Deacon had been brought in during the early 1840s as a young engineer. He served the firm until 1851 when he set up in business in Widnes as a chemical manufacturer. Douglas Herman, a product of the Royal College of Chemistry in London, was another such recruit. Pilkington had written to them in 1870 for 'a German if possible' and Herman had been recommended as 'a young Englishman though of German extraction ... a clever young fellow of original thought'. He started at £150 a year and reached £1,000 at the end of 1892, soon after he had drawn the partners' attention to the plate glass factory at Maubeuge.

Manchester University Chemistry School provided two graduates early in the present century who were to become key figures on the technical side between the wars. R. F. Taylor, who had taken a First before going on to graduate work in Berlin, reached Pilkington in 1905. R. B. LeMare took an M.Sc in Chemistry at Manchester before spending some time in America. He wanted to return to England and, 'evidently a very clever man and very highly recommended', he started work with the company in 1907. University College, Sheffield, provided a third technical recruit of note, F. B. Waldron, who joined the firm in 1911 as head of the drawing office at Cowley Hill. He developed the intricate continuous grinding and polishing plant at Cowley Hill, the great feat of engineering skill mentioned in the previous chapter.

The years just before 1914 also witnessed the arrival of other particularly valuable recruits, some of whom were eventually to reach the board in Cozens-Hardy's time. We have also mentioned R. M. Weeks, the Cambridge Natural Sciences graduate who had captained the university football team, joined the company in 1911 and, after distinguished war service, became Cowley Hill works manager in 1920 and a director eight years later. He became Cozens-Hardy's deputy and succeeded him briefly as Pilkington's chairman in 1939. But the Second World War took him off to even more distinguished service: he became Deputy Chief of the Imperial General Staff

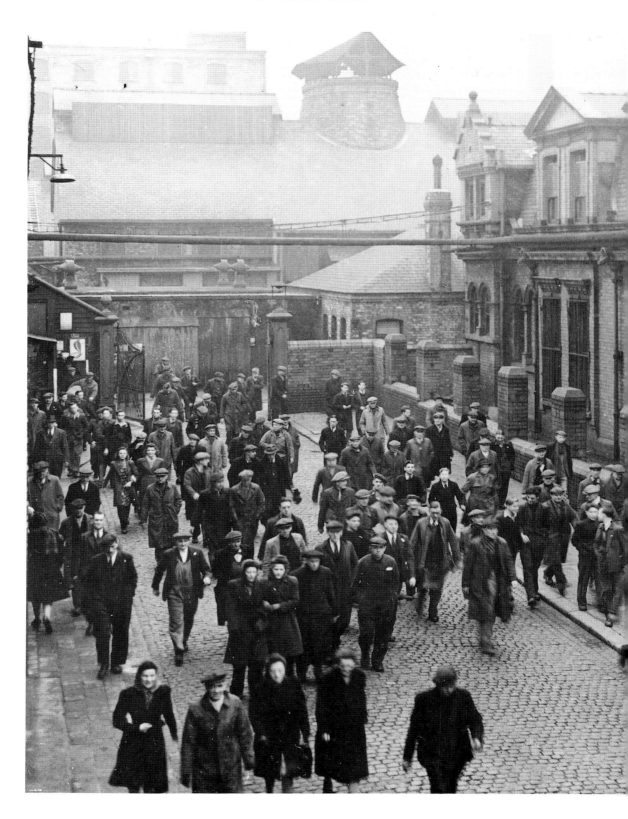

in 1941 and was knighted two years later. When the war was over, he did not return to St Helens but became a director, and later chairman, of Vickers Ltd as well as a director of a host of other companies. He was created Baron Weeks of Ryton in 1956.

Perhaps an even more important source of managerial talent than the universities was Allan Glen's School at Glasgow which specialized in scientific and technical courses. The medical officer appointed by Pilkington before the First World War was James Rutherford Kerr, eldest son of the headmaster there. He was followed to St Helens before 1914 by three more of its products, two of whom, P. M. Hogg and James Meikle, had subsequently trained as electrical engineers. The former was to become the firm's electrical engineer and the latter, in due course, Cowley Hill works manager and then, from 1939 to 1951, the company's production director. Another pre-war recruit from Allan Glen's was J. B. Watt who, as we have seen, was to be responsible for the successful development of the PPG flat drawn sheet glass process during the 1930s. He became Sheet Works works manager from 1936, a local director from 1938 and the company's production director from 1953 until his retirement in 1961. This remarkable flow of talented Scots from Allan Glen's by no means exhausted its contribution to Pilkington's management. There were to follow in later years P. L. Robson, the company's accountant, and

(LEFT): Factory workers leaving Grove Street c.1940. The head office can be seen on the right of the picture.

THE EXPANSION OF PILKINGTON

(ABOVE): Pilkington's first central research laboratory in Watson Street, St Helens, opened by Sir William Bragg in October 1938.

(ABOVE): Extension to the 1887 head office, designed by Herbert J. Rowse, opened in 1940.

The considerable growth of the business and the development of a committed structure called for a larger head office and research laboratories in the early 1960s.

(ABOVE): The imposing 12-storey glass-clad office block in pleasant, landscaped surroundings at Ravenhead opened in 1961. The new complex included the Pilkington Glass Museum, the single-storey building jutting out on the left.

(RIGHT): The large new research and development laboratories, built on a green field site at Lathom, about 10 miles from St Helens, opened in 1961.

J. H. Pemberton   *Raymond Robinson*

In the post-war years, Pilkington continued to rely heavily upon their agents overseas to manage their glass manufacturing and processing operations. Among them were J. H. Pemberton (Australia), Raymond Robinson (New Zealand), O. J. C. W. Breakspear (South Africa) and V. German (Canada).

O. J C. W. Breakspear   *V. German*

(ABOVE): *The rolling process involves squeezing semi-molten glass between metal rollers to produce a ribbon of controlled thickness and surface pattern.*

(ABOVE): *Float glass manufacture at Pilkington Glass Ltd, St Helens.*

(LEFT): *Raw materials for making float glass being fed automatically into the furnace.*

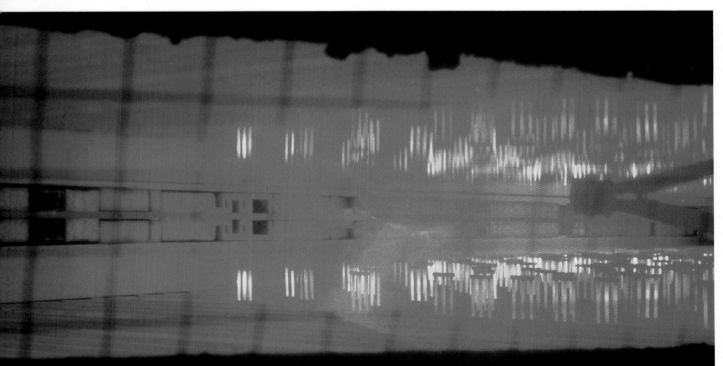

(ABOVE): *View inside the float bath where the ribbon of glass is floated across molten tin at over 1,000°C.*

(ABOVE): *Pilkington Glass Ltd's planar system allows complete façades to be glazed uninterrupted by frames – for exampl[e]
the impressive atrium of Judiciary Square in Washington DC, USA.*

(ABOVE): *The Galerias Pacifico in Buenos Aires, Argentina – an office building reborn as a shopping mall with 4,000m² of VASA float glass.*

(ABOVE): *The Bergianska project built in Stockholm, Sweden – a hothouse in a botanical garden using Pilkington K Glass and the planar glazing system.*

(ABOVE): *The British Pavilion in Seville, designed and built specifically for Spain's Expo '92 exhibition.*

(ABOVE): *Triplex rear windscreens on the Nissan Sunderland track ...*

... and in the Nissan Micra, the European Car of the Year 1993.

(ABOVE): *The 1993 Z28 Camaro with Libbey-Owens-Ford Co.'s new tinted Galaxsee, privacy glass with solar control.*

(ABOVE): *The SSC Radisson Diamond – a twin-hulled cruise ship extensively glazed by the marine division of Finland's Lamino Oy.*

(LEFT): *Pilkington Aerospace produces framed, heated windscreens for the X2000, Sweden's high-speed tilting train.*

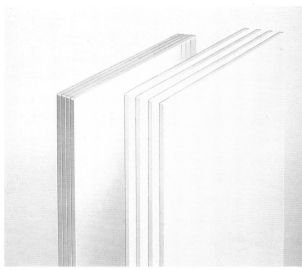

(ABOVE): *Pyrostop is a fire protection glass used mainly as a building product. It consists of several sheets of glass, separated by special fire-resisting intumescent layers. On exposure to fire, these layers expand to form an opaque, rigid shield which provides protection against radiant heat.*

(LEFT): *The Frankfurt AM Main in Germany glazed with Flachglas AG's Radarstop, a coated glass designed to reduce radar interference from buildings near airports.*

George McOnie who was to become its time-study specialist, Doncaster and Cowley Hill works manager and eventually a director. Against this impressive roll of Glasgow-educated talent, Edinburgh provided James Jex-Blake Forbes, an engineering graduate who, having worked at Cowley Hill from 1921, became manager of the new Triplex (Northern) works at Eccleston from 1930.

Other senior posts came to be occupied by local men who also worked their way up inside the company. F. E. Slocombe, son of a Pilkington employee, himself originally apprenticed to a fitter and turner, became works manager at Doncaster and then local director at a salary of £2,500. (He retired in 1938 on a pension of £1,000 a year after fifty-one years with the company.) J. H. Dickinson, son of the firm's legal agent, later took over the legal department and served as a director from 1931 to 1937. The other new non-family director of 1931 was W. S. Tunnock, son of the company's Glasgow agent, who had served as company secretary from 1920.

Pilkington's trainee scheme, started in 1933, included both outside recruits and internal candidates. One of the former, G. E. Beer, who had joined the company shortly before, attracted by the prospect of a traineeship, was to become in due course Head of Group Personnel Services. O. J. Breakspear (a Cambridge graduate), L. O. Gallon, J. H. Pemberton, and R. Robinson (all staff recruits) were to feature prominently in the company's growing activities abroad after 1945. None of the trainees of the 1930s, however, was to reach the main board at St Helens; but all the successful ones had important parts to play, along with other non-family recruits, in the remarkable post-war growth of the company.

PART TWO

5

Significant Post-War Developments

Pilkington's factories at St Helens escaped virtually unscathed from the wartime air raids even though Manchester and Merseyside, which lay on each side of the town, suffered considerable damage. The relative immunity of St Helens was just as well, for German raids greatly increased the demand for British glass, the building material most vulnerable to bombing. The company subsequently claimed, with some pride, 'that London was twice reglazed, and at one period three million square feet of glass per week was sent to the London area'. Pilkington home sales of sheet glass were 50 per cent higher in volume than they had been in 1938 and the company was also able to increase its export trade to markets abroad which could no longer be supplied from continental Europe. Again, it was sheet glass that benefited most: exports rose in 1941 to nearly three times their volume in 1938, Pilkington's best pre-war year.

New selling arrangements were made with dealers at home during the war so as to be the better able to meet foreign competition when the war was over. In earlier times, when all window glass was hand blown, the larger sheets had cost more to produce and were, therefore, sold at higher prices. This was no longer the case with continuous machine production; but the Belgians still sold their glass on the old

basis and, as they were the market leaders in the 1930s, Pilkington had no alternative but to follow suit. During the Second World War, however, it took the opportunity of the absence of Belgian competition to relate price to cost. It also cut distribution costs by increasing loose load deliveries of glass by road in stock sizes to main merchants, thus avoiding the expense of packing in wooden crates. These larger merchants were also equipped to perform many other processing functions, such as silvering for mirror manufacture and edge working for shelves. They often had showrooms. In recognition of these greater commitments and higher overheads, they received greater discounts on Pilkington's national price list (or tariff); but these discounts, which ranged up to about 20 per cent for plate glass and 5, 15 and 15 per cent for sheet, were so arranged that the highest level was relatively easy to achieve in terms of turnover. At the same time, the function of Pilkington's own depots was changed. Set up in the later nineteenth century to discourage the sale of foreign glass, they were in future to act only as reserve stockists and to supply customers with whom the company retained direct accounts; and they remained the centre of operations for Pilkington's local sales force.

These changes in selling arrangements

stood Pilkington in good stead after 1945. Rather surprisingly in view of their location, most of the continental glassworks also escaped serious damage and were soon hard at work again. Sales to Britain, however, for many years fell to a mere 10 per cent of total sales in the British market. This was a far cry from the 1930s when foreign sheet glass sales equalled those of British manufacture. In a world crying out for flat glass, the continentals sold their product elsewhere.

Immediately after the war, Pilkington's main concern was to absorb returning servicemen as soon as possible, to recruit others – especially engineers – and to increase its production of flat glass. A new five-machine sheet glass tank came into use at St Helens at the end of 1946 and, at the government's insistence, the next new tank, with four machines, was located at Pontypool. Additional output was obtained by further improvement of the PPG process: by increasing ribbon speed and diminishing production losses. In the other branches of flat glass, too – polished plate and rolled plate – the machines were run at higher speeds to meet the insistent market demand; and, as Pilkington sought licensees for its plate glass twin grinder, it continued to give high priority to maintaining technical supremacy in this branch of the industry.

Apart from flat glass, which was the mass-production money-maker, Pilkington did not regard its other items of manufacture with much favour. They were made at a works that had been acquired from a former competitor at Ravenhead, some distance from its own factories at Grove Street and Cowley Hill, and consisted of items such as wireless accumulators (hardly a winner with the spread of mains-powered radios), glass insulators and glass bricks (manufactured under licence). This aptly, but rather disparagingly, named Miscellaneous

Department did not endear itself any more to the directors by consistently losing money, though they kept it running in the hope that it would sooner or later break even. Unlike Chance Brothers, Pilkington concentrated almost exclusively on flat glass.

In 1945, however, as we have noted, Pilkington became majority shareholder in Chance; and with Chance came glass fibres, about to be developed on a much larger scale, and optical glass, in which Pilkington and Chance had already collaborated during the war in a small shadow factory at St Helens, Umbroc. Here were opportunities to diversify and to become more like competitors abroad, such as St Gobain, PPG and Asahi, which had interests in chemicals and paints and had already become concerned with glass fibres, or were about to do so. Such seemed the profit and possibilities of flat glass, however, that Pilkington may not have seen the opportunities for diversification that Chance presented to its purchaser. Reluctance to diversify remained a primary tenet of belief for Harry Pilkington even so late as 1969. Addressing the first Group Conference that year, he remarked:

> I hope that no one will feel that this deliberate policy of keeping ourselves to the things that we really know about … that are going to tax our abilities to the full, is a real restraint or that there is any need to look for extraneous excursions. We are always receiving requests to help someone or other to start manufacturing something or other, somewhere. We must have turned down at least 99 per cent of these. I think there are very few indeed of those that we will regret having turned down.

He did, however, go on immediately to make one important proviso:

I am sure that the policy set out, while not necessarily right for all time, is one that is right for the next few years, unless we are compelled by aggressive action of competitors to amend it as part of a general, uneconomic and unprofitable war.

Aggressive action, therefore, was something that Pilkington bent over backwards to avoid. Glassmaking had become a heavily capitalized industry, dominated internationally by fewer than ten major groups operating (to quote Harry Pilkington again) 'exceptionally large units in relation to demand ... There are few, if any, other industries in such a position.' This being the case, he concluded:

I want everybody to accept that peace among the very big manufacturers, of whom we are not the biggest, can only be obtained by a spirit of mutual sacrifice and mutual trust; that it is for me and others to get the other manufacturers constantly to remember that for themselves. It is for me to ask you from time to time to forgo opportunities or to make sacrifices that are quite considerable in the short term in the interests of the very much longer prosperity of the whole industry, to exercise patience sometimes and to turn the other cheek sometimes. As well as sometimes to take opportunities quickly when they come ... we must forgo temporary advantages and accept temporary irritations in order to have a prosperous industry generally, of which we are a fully respected part.

This Christian outlook served Pilkington well during Harry Pilkington's chairmanship between 1949 and 1973. The future Lord Pilkington – one of the outstanding business leaders of his day – and his fellow directors had the good fortune to gain unprecedented power and influence in the glassmaking world by achieving technical ascendancy over all Pilkington's rivals. The company was in a position to apply his benevolent philosophy in a less charitable world.

Lord Pilkington's successors were not so fortunate. The remarkable new technology developed during Harry Pilkington's chairmanship was to lead to the very aggressive action he had worked so hard to avoid, for the new technology (the float process) made overproduction all the easier in an industry that relied so heavily on two markets, building and the motor industry, both soon to undergo simultaneous cyclical depressions at the beginning of the 1980s and again after 1989.

To add to Pilkington's anxieties, the company, having gone public in 1970, by about 1980 found itself particularly accountable to powerful institutional shareholders, notably insurance companies, keen on regular returns on their investment. The transition was to some extent cushioned by income from float glass royalties and licence fees; but, insofar as these were ploughed back into the acquisition of major flat glass producers in the United States and on the continent of Europe and into the building of more float plants in the Nordic countries, South America and in the Commonwealth, this only made the company more vulnerable to cyclical downswings in building and motor manufacture.

Pilkington's history since the later 1940s may be conveniently divided into three periods which happen to coincide with the tenure of its chairmen: Lord Pilkington (1949–1973) and Sir Antony Pilkington (1980–), with Sir Alastair Pilkington FRS holding the chairmanship for the seven years between 1973 and 1980 during the transition from the buoyant years of full employment and family ownership to the recent and more difficult times.

The fourth generation of Pilkington, who, as has been seen, were put through their paces during the Cozens-Hardy regime of the 1930s, found themselves in charge of the business in the later 1940s. Geoffrey Pilkington, who had held the fort during the war and stayed on for some years after it when Sir Ronald Weeks did not return to St Helens, handed over as chairman of the executive committee in 1947 to Douglas Phelps, a staff officer during the war. The chairmanship of the company, which Geoffrey Pilkington had held since 1932, passed to Harry Pilkington two years later, in 1949.

Harry Pilkington, who had a very good head for figures, had been a member of Cozens-Hardy's finance committee from its creation in 1936. He had also been in charge of sales since then and had been responsible for the new sales organization introduced during the war. As company chairman he took charge of financial affairs generally and represented Pilkington on various national bodies. This soon led to his becoming chairman of the Federation of British Industries (now the Confederation, CBI) between 1953 and 1955 (knighted 1953), a director of the Bank of England from 1955, chairman of committees (notably on broadcasting) and of the Royal Commission on Doctors' and Dentists' Remuneration. Arthur Pilkington, who had rejoined the Coldstream Guards at the outbreak of war, returned with an MC and took over the sales side of the business; Harry's younger brother, Lawrence, took charge of research. They, together with the other family members, Roger Percival and the Hon. H. A. (Peter) Cozens-Hardy, and J. B. Watt, the non-family member who had played such a notable part in developing the PPG process at Grove Street and joined the Executive in 1949, formed a remarkable, complementary, top management team. (John Tilbury and James Meikle, the other

non-family members, retired in 1950 and 1951 respectively.) David Frost Pilkington (born 1925), Guy Pilkington's son and the youngest member of the fourth Pilkington generation, read Engineering at Cambridge before doing his two years' National Service in the RNVR. He joined the company in 1947 on the production side and became a member of the executive committee in 1957.

Lionel Alexander Bethune (Alastair) Pilkington, who was to invent the float glass process, came to join this team by an extraordinary accident. Richard Pilkington, a family shareholder but not a director, lost his seat as MP for Widnes in the Labour landslide of 1945, and began to occupy his spare time taking an interest in the Pilkington family tree, in the course of which he happened to get in touch with Alastair's father, Colonel Lionel Pilkington, a businessman in Reading. Having established the fact that their researches had not been able to find any traceable link between the two families (though some of Colonel Lionel's forebears could claim a Yorkshire background), they got round to discussing the rising generation. Alastair, Lionel's second son, having volunteered for the army while at university, fought in the war and been taken prisoner, was then back at Cambridge completing his Mechanical Sciences tripos and would, in two years' time, be looking for a job. Would Pilkington be interested? The company was indeed interested, for engineers were in short supply. The board minute on the subject is most illuminating in many ways, not least because of the view the glassmaking Pilkingtons took of the family and the reprimand which Richard Pilkington received for his help:

The Directors considered a report furnished by Colonel Phelps of an

(LEFT): Douglas Vandeleur Phelps (1904–1988).

Douglas Phelps, son of a Pilkington daughter who had married J. V. Phelps, came into the business in 1927 and assisted R. M. Weeks on the manufacturing side. He also became a director in 1934. He was mobilised with the Territorial Army in 1939, went to the Staff College, Camberley, the following year and served in staff appointments in various parts of the world. Returning to Pilkington after the war, he became chairman of the executive committee from 1947 to 1965.

(RIGHT): Arthur Cope Pilkington (1909–1981).

Arthur Cope Pilkington joined Pilkington in 1934 from the Coldstream Guards where he had served for some years as a regular officer. He did a spell on the sales side, and as agent in South Africa, and returned to the Guards during the war and was awarded the MC in 1945. He came back to Pilkington and served as commercial director responsible for exports. He was soon pressing for the decentralization of the company's administrative structure and when he succeeded Douglas Phelps as chairman of its executive committee between 1965 and 1967, he saw to it that this process was started.

Llavallol, Argentina.

Pilkington's first factories abroad were built in the Commonwealth during the 1930s to toughen or laminate glass exported from Britain. The last thing the company wished to do was to manufacture glass itself outside its British factories, for this would reduce the loading of its machines at home and push up costs. It was, however, obliged to build a sheet and rolled glass factory in 1938 at Llavallol, near Buenos Aires, in collaboration with St Gobain and other European producers, in order to defend the market there from Argentine competition. After the war, the South African government brought pressure to bear on Pilkington to manufacture there. Production started at Springs, 30 miles from Johannesburg, in 1951. And when Pittsburgh Plate Glass acquired a factory in Canada for sheet glass manufacture, Pilkington had to respond with its own plant at Scarborough, a suburb of Toronto, which also came into production in 1951. Three years later, a fourth glassmaking venture followed at Asansol in Bengal, undertaken jointly with the Hindustan Development Corporation. Other safety glass plants were built and existing ones extended; but not for manufacturing polished plate glass, which continued to be exported from St Helens.

Port Elizabeth, South Africa., which processed Pillkington's British-made glass.

Scarborough, Canada.

Asansol, Bengal.

interview which he and Mr W. H. Pilkington had had with Colonel Lionel G. Pilkington on the subject of his second son, Alastair, joining the PB organisation after completing his studies at University. The matter had arisen from an almost casual introduction by Mr Richard Pilkington. The Directors felt that it should be pointed out to Mr Richard Pilkington that the method of introduction was very irregular.

Mr L. G. Pilkington's branch of the family broke away at least 15 generations ago [i.e. as far back as the St Helens Pilkingtons' family tree went]. It was agreed that a member of the Pilkington Family, however remote, could be accepted only as a potential Family Director. After considerable discussion the Board agreed that, in principle, they were prepared to open the door wider to really promising candidates.

Mr A. C. (Cecil) Pilkington [who had given up active management in 1931 and lived near Oxford] pointed out that our business is largely in the North of England, that conditions of life in the North of England are very different from those in the South, and we must be very sure that a potential candidate brought up in the South understands and is willing to take on the obligation of living in the North, both for himself and his family.

It was also emphasised that the private nature of PB's business, which has had great advantages for both employers and workpeople, demands a high standard from the Directors, and in the political conditions of the future will probably do so to an even greater extent. If we are to throw the net wider, we must take applicants only of the very highest standard.

With regard to the particular case under discussion, it was considered that before any action in respect of Alastair Pilkington was taken, we should take steps to learn more about Colonel L. G. Pilkington – in particular his business and family background. He is Managing Director of the Pulsometer Engineering Co., Reading, which Lord Cozens-Hardy pointed out was a small but well established company, he believed of Quaker origin.

These enquiries were obviously reassuring and in due course Alastair was brought up to St Helens to spend three days at the various works and to meet all the members of the executive. In March 1947, the board, having received favourable reports from the works managers and technical directors, were prepared to offer him a family traineeship. He started work at St Helens in the following August as a technical assistant ('an unusual status for an ex-officer', he recalls) and his first job was on gas producers, where pokers six feet long were needed to clear the clinker ('quite rugged'). He was soon involved, however, in experimental work at Cowley Hill before being sent in 1950 to Doncaster, as production manager. With James Meikle's unexpected retirement in 1951, soon after Alastair Pilkington's return to St Helens, he found his promotion even further accelerated. He joined the executive committee at the beginning of 1953, at the age of thirty-two.

In the meantime the executive had been obliged to start glassmaking in South Africa and Canada. As in Argentina, Pilkington became involved in manufacture there in order to hold a valuable market against the threat of competing local production; but in South Africa and Canada, Pilkington had to provide all the capital and skill itself, not in company with other European glassmakers. Apart from the drain on its resources when much expansion was taking place at home, Pilkington was most reluctant to manufacture outside the United Kingdom, since production of raw glass (as distinct

Selwyn House, Cleveland Row, St James's, overlooking Green Park, which became Pilkington's London headquarters from January 1950.

from the processing, at its safety glass plants abroad, of raw glass exported from the United Kingdom) reduced the loading on the machines at home and, therefore, their profitability. The South African government, however, threatened to admit another manufacturer if Pilkington did not put down a factory itself. After much foot-dragging, this it eventually had to do. The sheet glass factory was opened at Springs, thirty miles to the east of Johannesburg, in 1951.

The company was even more reluctant to make glass in Canada in view of the earlier fiasco with the drawn cylinder process at Thorold; but when powerful Pittsburgh Plate Glass acquired a previously uneconomic sheet glass plant there, Pilkington was obliged to respond. The Pilkington factory was opened at Scarborough, a suburb of Toronto, also in 1951. In addition, sheet glass manufacture was started at Asansol, India, in 1954. This, however, was a joint venture with the Hindustan Development Corporation, undertaken because Pilkington believed that 'in some way or another a footing in this market (which will be fairly big one day, it is thought) should be obtained'. Although these three factories were at the expense of orders for sheet glass from St Helens, they did not affect exports of the more expensive product, polished plate. This heavy investment abroad was nevertheless starting to transform Pilkington into an international company, not one which merely traded inter-nationally. And, by 1954, pilot plant experiments were taking place at St Helens which were destined to transform Pilkington into an international company on a far greater scale.

6

Floating Windows

The twin grinder had given Pilkington technical ascendancy in plate glass manufacture before the war. Twin-ground glass, with its splendid parallel surfaces, had been launched in Britain in 1939. It had already been licensed the year before to St Gobain for use in France, French territories abroad, Germany, Italy and Spain; but St Gobain had difficulty in working the long line of grinding heads. Useful royalties were not received until after the war. Further licences were taken out by Glaver in Belgium in 1950 and Libbey–Owens–Ford in 1951. Pittsburgh Plate Glass eventually took one out in December 1954. A twin polisher, however, proved more difficult to develop; in the final stage, therefore, the ribbon had to be passed under a succession of polishing heads, one side at a time. The process was still not completely continuous.

Although the twin grinder was hailed as a great technical feat, it was a feat of engineering rather than of glassmaking. The whole plant – tank furnace, annealing lehr, twin grinder and polishers – stretched out in a line no less than 1,400 feet long. Contemporaries noted (whether with pride or regret is not clear) that this was seventy feet longer than the *Queen Mary*, then the largest ship afloat. The fixed capital costs of electric motors and machinery were enormous. The running costs were also considerable. A supply of electricity amounting to 1,500 kilowatts was needed to grind 10 per cent off each side of the plate glass ribbon as it emerged from the lehr, not to mention the cost of the extra fuel and raw materials needed to produce the surplus glass in the first place. The resulting planimetry may have been beautiful to behold – but was there no means of achieving the same result with less wasteful expenditure?

This was a question discussed by the Manufacturing Conference, a body set up in January 1947 by James Meikle, then Pilkington's senior production director. It met monthly and at its March meeting of that year, Meikle was asking whether the time had not arrived at which attempts to produce an effective twin polisher should be abandoned and efforts be made to discover a new method of producing glass of plate glass quality without any costly grinding and polishing. A team of engineers was formed to look into this. It first explored the use of vibrating platens, or plates, as a substitute for grinding and polishing, an invention of the Director of Research at the Owens–Illinois Glass Co., Toledo, Ohio. Although this quest eventually proved fruitless, Pilkington had nevertheless identified the part of its

operations which, if changed, would yield the greatest economic return. It exemplified, too, the merits of Harry Pilkington's belief in 'keeping ourselves to things we really know about'.

Pilkington, then, was already thinking about means of replacing grinding and polishing when Alastair Pilkington joined the company. Although he was posted to Doncaster as production manager in 1949 when the experiments with platens began at St Helens, the need to discover the best means of handling the still soft ribbon of glass emerging from the platens introduced him to the idea of floating a ribbon of glass over a surface of molten metal. Experiments on the use of tin as a carrier at a temperature of about 600°C were, in fact, carried out by another young engineer, Kenneth Bickerstaff. There was no question at that time, however, of *forming* the ribbon over the molten tin at the far higher temperature of about 1,000°C.

Soon after his return to St Helens, however, Alastair had his brainwave, the possibility of linking the two: floating the ribbon down the bath of molten tin through a temperature gradient starting at 1,000°C and ending at around 600°C at which it could be carried forward on rollers. Alastair made this suggestion at one of the regular meetings of the Manufacturing Conference. As the work on platens was not making much progress, the engineering team was instructed to explore what came to be known by its code name: the LAB project (Alastair's initials).

The obstacles to success were formidable, not least the need to keep the surface of the tin absolutely level and the atmosphere above it completely neutral. As Alastair Pilkington later recalled: 'If we had realized all the horrors which lay ahead, we would never have started.' The scientists working in Pilkington's central research laboratory did realize the horrors.

They prophesied failure and missed few opportunities to disparage what they saw as an impossible quest. The engineers, however, proceeded by trial and error and, as no one fault seemed incapable of correction, pressed on regardless, ably led on the spot by the team leader, Richard Barradell-Smith (ex-Rolls Royce, with a first-class degree from Glasgow University and further qualifications from the Massachusetts Institute of Technology) and supervized by the inventor himself, soon able to plead his case on the executive itself and as a board member. Three small-scale pilot plants produced promising, but by no means conclusive, results. In the spring of 1955 the board nevertheless authorized a full-scale production unit.

This was a very courageous and extremely risky decision; Pilkington was putting all its faith in what was then an untried and radically new method of making flat glass. If it succeeded, this branch of the industry would benefit from the greatest leap forward in the whole of its history. On the other hand, the penalty of failure was enormous, for Pilkington was then in need of an additional plate glass line to meet the rapidly growing demand. The lure of the unknown depended entirely on the large cost saving that it promised: a fixed capital cost then estimated at a mere £65,000 compared with the millions a new plate glass line of *Queen Mary* dimensions would cost; and glass produced at an estimated 10*d* per square foot instead of 1*s* 9*d*.

The float tank at Cowley Hill (CH1) was lit on 6 May 1957. The auguries were not good. It had already cost £676,000. The critics wagged their fingers when it did not make a single square foot of saleable glass for month after month, fifteen months in all. The company sustained huge losses; and when Harry Pilkington was eventually able to announce float glass to the world on 20 January 1959, he had to admit that the quantity of the new glass then produced, though 'quite considerable', was 'not yet enough to be offered freely'. (Triplex, in which Pilkington was by then the majority shareholder, was the only original buyer.) During the year ended 31 March 1959 £903,000 more was lost and a further, though smaller, loss of £525,000 occurred in the following financial year, 1959/60.

More development of the process was needed. In particular, glass much thinner than quarter-inch (all that could be made at first) had to be produced before American and other manufacturers were prepared to take out licences, for the thinner variety was essential for the manufacture of laminated safety glass. The first licence was not issued until July 1962; and only in the financial year ended March 1963, when the second float line (CH4) came into use at St Helens, did the new product bring a steady profit to the company. Pilkington was able to discontinue plate glass production in 1967. By 1970 there were already twenty-eight float glass units operating abroad, including two by Pilkington in Canada.

It is clear that this remarkable leap in the dark, decided upon in 1955, would never have been brought to ultimate success, even with the indispensable resources of the company and the know-how of its glassmakers, without two very favourable conditions.

The economic climate of the time was very encouraging. World demand for glass, for use both in the very rapidly growing motor industry and for building, grew fast. Pilkington's pre-tax profits – £3,187,000 in 1951/52 – after falling to half that sum in the difficult year 1952/53, then rose to higher levels of £4,584,000, £5,760,000 and £5,180,000 in the three subsequent years. The timing of the major

float investment decision in 1955 was particularly favourable. In May of that year, world demand for glass reached famine proportions: customers as far inland as Chicago, for instance, were offering Pilkington long-term contracts if it could only meet their immediate needs. The decision to embark upon the full-scale production unit was, therefore, taken in the warm glow of considerable economic prosperity. Although 1956/57 was not so remunerative (pre-tax profits fell to £4,371,000), the profit in 1957/58 (£4,190,000) took account of the very considerable losses on the full-scale float production plant. In 1958/59, despite the further float loss of £900,000, pre-tax profits of £5,594,000 were reported and in the following year £8,599,000.

The company did not have to incur any additional debt to produce these results. During the decade as a whole, the company's total borrowings did not rise above £1,000,000, although the capital employed in the business trebled, rising from £17 million to over £48 million. The financing of float, that is to say, was easily met out of current earnings and deprived the company of less than a fifth of its profit even in the worst year, 1957/58 – and less than that if the alternative, the much more costly plate glass line, had been embarked upon. The shareholders, under fifty of them and almost all family, appeared to be unperturbed by the heavy development costs involved.

The second favourable – and perhaps vital – condition for the ultimate success of float was Alastair Pilkington's presence on the board, where he could plead its case at the highest level. He is a superb advocate and, once convinced of a particular course of action could, like any good advocate, plead convincingly even when those in favour of giving up and saving further expenditure seemed to have a powerful

THE FLOAT PROCESS

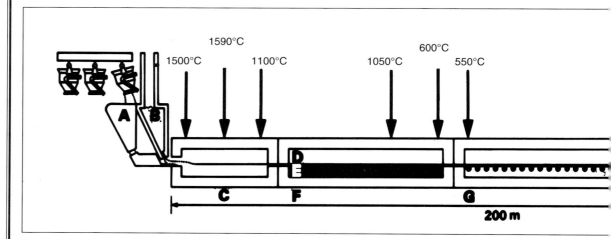

A diagram of the process

Handblowing of sheet glass and the intermittent manufacture of cast plate glass were mechanized and made continuous during the first half of the present century, Pilkington playing a leading role in the latter in collaboration with the Ford Motor Co. of Detroit.

The float process, the invention of Sir Alastair Pilkington, was something fundamentally new. It was first announced by the company in 1959 and, after further development, licensed throughout the world. It cut costs to such an extent that it quickly replaced plate glass manufacture and, with further development, came to be made cheaply enough to replace sheet glass, too. Float glass factories are quiet places remotely controlled from monitor screens.

(i) The ribbon emerging from the lehr ...

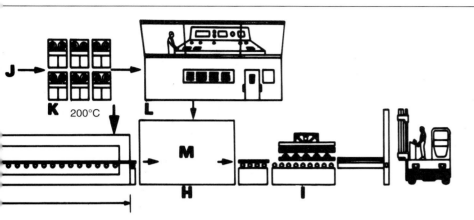

A	Raw material mix	**I**	Automatic stacking
B	Cullet	**J**	Orders
C	Oil-fired melting furnace	**K**	Computers
D	Controlled atmosphere	**L**	Control point
E	Molten tin	**M**	Computers govern the cutting processes, matching complex orders to the continuous ribbon of glass, and directing
F	Float bath		
G	Annealing lehr		
H	Automatic warehouse (not shown)		

the cut glass to the appropriate part of the warehouse for stacking and dispatch. The automatic warehouse stands by itself as a major advance in glass technology.

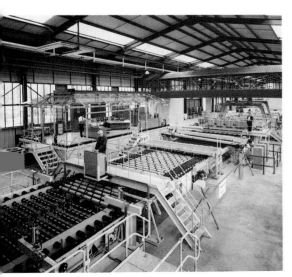

(ii) ... It then proceeds along the float line to an automated warehouse where it is cut to the required size and distributed for packing.

(iii) The automatic cutting station viewed from the control room at the end of the float line.

Alastair Pilkington (far left) demonstrating the distortion-free quality of a small piece of float glass to (on his left) E. Litherland, production manager, Cowley Hill, George Dickinson, development manager, J. E. C. Thomas, tanks manager, Jack Topping, special examiner and Richard Barradell-Smith (ex-Rolls Royce), leader of the float development team.

Three small pilot plants produced promising results and in the Spring of 1955 – a highly profitable period for the company – Pilkington authorized a full-scale production unit which was started up in May 1957. The theoretical problems involved were formidable and many of the scientists in the company forecast failure; but the engineers pressed on and Alastair Pilkington, a member of the executive committee from 1953, was able to plead their case very logically and persuasively to the other directors. The chairman, Sir Harry Pilkington, gave him every support. Even so, Alastair needed all his considerable powers of advocacy as the plant produced tons and tons of unsaleable glass for 15 months. Float glass was first announced to the world on 20 January 1959. Further development was needed before the first licence was issued in July 1962. Pilkington was able to discontinue the manufacture of plate glass in 1967 and other manufacturers elsewhere in the world soon followed suit.

case. Such unflagging conviction on the part of the inventor, in constant touch with the development team, was crucial to ultimate success, especially in view of the large waves of doubt emanating from the expert scientists who appreciated only too well *theoretically* the problems with which the engineers were confronted. Of crucial importance, too, was the constant support of the chairman, Harry Pilkington. No lover of the motto 'safety first', he never lost his nerve even when the news was bad and the criticisms most shrill; and there were no large outside shareholders to hold him back.

It would be a mistake to underestimate either of these favourable circumstances. If the economic climate had been less propitious – if the pilot plant experiments had taken place in the 1960s, for instance – it is highly unlikely that the costly production unit would have been authorized in the first place. Similarly, if Alastair Pilkington had not, to Pilkington's great advantage, been recruited when he was, and to have proved such an inventive engineer and able advocate, and if he had not been given accelerated promotion so that he could plead his case at director level, it is equally unlikely that the float process would have reached ultimate success.

There are those, too, who believe that if Pilkington had been a public company at the time and responsible to outside shareholders, there would have been no float process either. It would certainly have been more difficult to keep its development secret for so long; but with no outside shareholders, press curiosity was non-existent. The family and the many Pilkington employees had grown up with a tradition of keeping processes secret, a tradition inherited from the glassmakers of old.

The success of float glass put a very powerful weapon into Pilkington's hand.

Leslie Newton Wall

Leslie Newton Wall (born 1916), who joined Pilkington as assistant company solicitor in 1956, became much involved with Alastair Pilkington in the licensing of the float process. He became a director of the company in 1970.

Prestigious and profitable polished plate glass manufacture was obsolescent by the early 1960s. Pilkington abandoned it in 1967 and other major glass manufacturers soon followed. As more efficient float lines were developed, the cheaper sheet glass process was also destined to be threatened and replaced. Pilkington might have waged open war on all its competitors by trying to put down float lines in all the major glass manufacturing countries of the world. This, however, would have involved the raising of capital and start-up teams, far beyond the means of a private family concern; it would have been virtually impossible even for a public company which could have raised

The lower costs of float glass made it economic for Pilkington to put down float plants in markets abroad earlier than a more costly plate glassworks would have justified. In Canada, for instance, the first float line was added to the existing sheet glassworks at Scarborough in 1967, and a second in 1970. At Dandenong, Victoria, Australia, where a new sheet glassworks had been opened in 1963, a float line was added in 1974. No longer were Pilkington's manufacturing activities concentrated in Britain.

Scarborough in Canada, with added float line.

Dandenong in Australia.

outside share capital. In any case, it would certainly have caused the glass-making concerns threatened by such a hostile attack to seek political protection from their governments.

Pilkington gave much thought to the means of wielding its new weapon. It realized that lower fixed capital costs might encourage newcomers into an industry in which very high fixed capital costs had previously deterred new entrants. The existing coterie of fewer than ten major manufacturers competed strongly enough in their cyclical industry to ensure efficient production and adequate supplies in all years at prices that would produce enough revenue in good times to tide them over bad. Harry Pilkington, in particular, as we have seen,was a firm believer in friendly competition, not outright war: 'mutual sacrifice and mutual trust'.

Pilkington policy on float licensing was, therefore, to license the existing major producers and not to put them at a disadvantage by licensing newcomers. At the same time, Pilkington encouraged its licensees to assist in the further development of float by granting them free use of any improvements they might make on condition that these were also available for use by Pilkington itself. Leslie Wall, who had joined Pilkington's Legal Department in 1956, played a crucial role in the devising of this ingenious licence and also in the negotiations with future licensees.

Lower fixed capital costs enabled Pilkington, with the aid of float royalties, to put down float plants in its export markets abroad earlier than it could have otherwise embarked upon a far costlier plate glass line. It thus secured a presence in flat glassmaking in countries other than South Africa and Canada (and also Australia and Argentina, where it was already involved in joint ventures). Among the first of these was Mexico, where Pilkington took a 35 per cent stake in the sheet glass manufacturer Vidrio Plano in 1965 in exchange for waiving part of the float glass licence fees.

7

Diversification – But Not at the Expense of Flat Glass

The successful development of float glass ensured Pilkington's continued, unrivalled primacy in flat glass during Harry Pilkington's chairmanship. The great extension of safety glass processing at home and abroad to meet the very rapidly growing motor industry demand, and the eventual control of Triplex, gave it an even greater share of Pilkington's operations. This brought (Sir) Barrie Heath, a wartime DFC, the dynamic managing director of Triplex from 1960 (and subsequently Triplex chairman), into Pilkington's top executive management, until he left to become chairman of GKN. (He remained for some further years as a non-executive Pilkington director.)

Despite this concentration on flat glass, opportunities for diversification arising from Chance's earlier non-flat glass interests continued to be pursued. Alan Hudson Davies, a science graduate with considerable business experience behind him with ICI and Bulmer's, was recruited in 1946 to take charge of a factory at Ravenhead for the *continuous* production of glass fibres, a process developed in the United States by Owens–Corning Fiberglas Corporation. His subsequent appointment as a Pilkington director in 1952 testified to the importance that Pilkington placed on its growing subsidiary, Fibreglass Ltd. A new factory for

glass textiles and fibres for glass-reinforced plastics, established at Possilpark, Glasgow, in 1948, soon proved too small. Glass reinforcement was moved to Valley Road, Birkenhead, in 1957, where disused works premises were renovated and re-equipped, and subsequently to a new, purpose-built works at Wrexham in 1971. Possilpark and Valley Road were then closed. Greater emphasis was placed upon glass fibre for thermal insulation.

Optical glass, a Chance staple product dating from the nineteenth century, stayed with the Chance side of the business until 1957, when optical and ophthalmic glass began to be made at a purpose-built factory on a greenfield site in the clear air at St Asaph in North Wales. Trading as the Chance–Pilkington Optical Works, the factory, Dr Lawrence Pilkington's particular concern, employed a continuous process licensed from the American Corning Glass Co. It soon became, *inter alia*, the largest producer of unpolished spectacle lens blanks in Europe. In 1966 Pilkington and Perkin Elmer Ltd, a subsidiary of the American multinational, joined forces at St Asaph to make optical and electro-optical systems for defence and other purposes. (It became Pilkington–PE in 1973 when Pilkington acquired the American shares.) The optical and ophthalmic side of

Pilkington's business was extended downstream towards the market when the Michael Birch Group, a holding company for ophthalmic opticians and manufacturers of microfilm equipment, was bought in 1974, followed by Barr & Stroud, the Scottish optical and precision engineers, in 1977.

At Ravenhead the previously un-attractive and unprofitable Miscellaneous Department took on a new lease of life with the manufacture of television tubes, needed in increasing quantities as transmitters spread from London in the later 1940s. When the manufacture of cathode ray bulbs (the glass part of cathode ray tubes) was discussed by the Pilkington executive on 8 March 1950, it was noted that BTH and GEC were not interested since they had their own source of supply, but that

Mullard, controlled by Philips of Eindhoven, were. The minutes record what, with hindsight, suggests a surprising reluctance to seize this particular opportunity. There was a discussion:

> on whether or not the manufacture of cathode ray bulbs, as at present designed, is our business, particularly so in view of the fact that..there is not yet any uniformity of requirements by all the television manufacturers and since these television manufacturers are still undecided as to what they really want.

Ravenhead was then making these glass bulbs by hand because it had difficulty in devising a continuous process.

Corning Glass of America, however, from which Pilkington had taken a licence to make

Sir Alan Hudson Davies (1901–1975)

Alan Meredyth Hudson Davies, a Cambridge Natural Sciences graduate, had been an industrial investigator with the National Institute of Industrial Psychology in the 1920s, an assistant commercial manager with ICI at Billingham (1928 –1933), then with Bulmer's cider, becoming works director from 1936, and chairman of the Birmingham District Manpower Board during the war before coming to Pilkington as managing director of the new factory of Fibreglass Ltd at Ravenhead, St Helens. He joined the Pilkington board in 1952. After his retirement as a full-time member of the Pilkington executive committee at the age of 65, in 1966, he chaired the board of governors of the United Liverpool Hospitals as well as involving himself in much other voluntary work. He received a knighthood in 1975 for his contribution to the health service.

glass bricks in the mid-1930s (and with which it was also linked more recently through the Owens–Corning Fiberglas Corporation) had already developed a continuous method of making television bulbs and was thinking of licensing it to J. A. Jobling of Sunderland, which already produced in Britain Corning's heat-resistant glass, sold under the trade name of Pyrex. Pilkington had also been obliged to take a share in Jobling when it had obtained the licence for glass bricks or blocks. When the executive discussed television bulbs again, in October 1950, it favoured their manufacture

Spreading the glass fibres into insulation mats.

Fibreglass was Pilkington's first major diversification out of flat glass. It came with the acquisition of Chance Brothers in and after 1936. Chance had first made glass fibres into glass silk under licence from Dr Pollak of Vienna at its rolled plate glass factory at Firhill, Glasgow, in 1930. It marketed the product as Idaglass, the insulating qualities being likened to those of eiderdown. But the Pollak method of drawing glass fibres did not prove very satisfactory; Chance was able to take a licence in April 1935 from Owens–Illinois for an improved continuous filament process which that American concern had developed. The Glasgow plant was extended and new plant installed there in 1937.

being concentrated at Sunderland. In the event, Jobling declined the Corning licence but, by May 1951, Ravenhead had devised a method of producing round 12″ bulbs continuously. By then, however, the state of the art had moved on and the market was demanding rectangular bulbs of 14″ and even 17″ diagonal which, for Ravenhead, as the executive ruefully reported, 'might be an extremely difficult pressing job'.

This proved to be the case, and in the favourable market conditions of January 1953, nearly three years after the possibilities of the television tube market were first discussed, Arthur Pilkington struck a more positive note: 'We should now decide that we are in the cathode tube market for good and not as a temporary measure – unless, of course, conditions and demand change considerably.'

Mullard was then planning a new factory near Blackburn for the manufacture of entire television sets and, in the next month, Arthur Pilkington reported that AEI, component suppliers but not themselves makers of sets, were prepared to buy up to half their needs from Ravenhead. Pilkington at last sought a licence from Corning and decided to put down a second tank exclusively for the manufacture of cathode ray tube glass. After teething troubles, the new arrangements came into use in the middle of 1955.

Ravenhead, however, ran into trouble a few years later when, after a dispute on Pilkington's prices, Mullard decided to put down a glassmaking facility of its own. This brought Pilkington and Siemens–Edison–Swan (part of AEI) closer together. At a meeting at AEI's office in London on 12 August 1959, Dr Aldington of SES put forward a remarkable proposal which, if successfully pursued, would have given Pilkington a foothold in a significant sector of the electronics industry. Pilkington's minute of that meeting records:

He [Dr Aldington] would like us to consider the possibility of going into a consortium with the set makers, SES, radio valve sections and PBs glassmaking. His idea is that the joint company would not make separate profits on the components but share the profit made on the whole operation of producing TV sets. We undertook to consider this as a possibility but pointed out that, as electronics were not our line, we would prefer to concentrate on glassmaking.

Pilkington again resisted the opportunity to diversify, though, in retrospect, AEI was far from being the right partner.

(Sir) Jules Thorn's business, however, then expanding rapidly, was a very different proposition. Thorn was an Austrian with a degree in business management from Vienna who had sold Austrian gas mantles in England before settling here as an importer of light bulbs and radio components. He then entered radio manufacture (Ferguson) in 1936, and developed the rental business. During the 1950s he had gone into fluorescent lighting in a big way and this had made him a major customer of glass tubing from Chance. In 1960 Thorn acquired Ultra radio and television, Philco and Pilot. In the following year the radio and television tube interests of AEI and Thorn Electrical Industries were merged. Pilkington thereafter found themselves having frequent, and often acrimonious, meetings with Thorn who then controlled half the country's television set-making capacity and was virtually Ravenhead's only customer for tubes. He proved a very awkward customer indeed. Pilkington did not venture further into television beyond the manufacture of the glass bulbs.

Pilkington was later approached by the Fairchild Camera and Instrument

(*LEFT*): Pilkington's other major diversification out of flat glass, unpolished spectacle lens blanks, also came via the acquisition of Chance Brothers which had specialized in optical – and especially lighthouse – work since the nineteenth century.

(*BELOW*): The Chance–Pilkington Optical Works was opened in a green field site at St Asaph in North Wales in 1957 – the air there was exceptionally clean. The particular concern of Dr Lawrence Pilkington, it soon became the largest producer of spectacle blanks in Europe employing a continuous process licensed by Pilkington from Corning Glass of America. In 1966 Pilkington, in collaboration with another American concern, Perkin Elmer, also began to manufacture electro-optical systems for defence and other purposes at St Asaph.

Dr Lawrence Herbert Austin Pilkington

Dr Lawrence Herbert Austin Pilkington (born 1911), Harry Pilkington's younger brother, having read Natural Sciences at Cambridge, joined Pilkington in 1935, and then the executive committee in 1940 as technical director. He was very much involved in the Society of Glass Technology at Sheffield University which awarded him an honorary doctorate in 1956.

Corporation, a high-tech American business with a turnover of $92 million, to set up a plant in Britain to make silicon transistors. This would considerably reduce the cost of making television sets (which still used valves) and put them two or three years ahead of Mullard. They were looking for someone who would supply the television tubes. Dr Lawrence Pilkington's response included the very definite statement of Pilkington's position: 'We are not in the electrical manufacturing business ...'

Pilkington even took the first opportunity to sell its interest in Jobling, manufacturers of Pyrex. When, in 1949, the main proprietor, E. J. Jobling-Purser, anxious to retire, offered his shares to Pilkington, as he was bound to do by previous agreement, Pilkington quickly sold them on to Thomas Tilling, noting that: 'experience with Jobling since the acquisition strengthens the view that there is very little common ground between the two companies and there is no real value to Pilkington in retaining Jobling'. This being the case, Pilkington had no hesitation in parting with Corning shares to Corning for its continuous television tube process in 1955 at a time of strict exchange control.

This extreme reluctance to diversify further out of flat glass – and its willingness to withdraw from heat-resistant ovenware – seems difficult to comprehend in the light of the company's subsequent difficulties arising from its over-dependence upon the two cyclical markets, motors and building. On the other hand, during the booming 1950s the company had little reason to foresee these troubles ahead; and the moves into manufacturing overseas would seem to be an insurance against any regional downturns in demand which, in Pilkington's experience in Britain, had not previously affected motors and building simultaneously.

Moreover, Pilkington's successful grasping of world supremacy in flat glass – achieved, perhaps, because of its almost single-minded concentration on the products it knew about – would seem an even greater guarantee for the future, provided it could maintain that lead. In any event, it was diversifying already into optical and ophthalmic glass, unaffected by the same cyclical fluctuations as flat glass, and into glass fibre.

Another important consideration needs to be borne in mind: the survival of Pilkington's extremely centralized administrative structure. Although Cozens-Hardy's committee system of the 1930s, extended somewhat after the war, did bring senior management into closer contact with the twelve or so members of the executive, these committees – the Manufacturing Conference, for instance – dealt with detail. The few members of the executive, mainly Pilkington family members, took all the policy decisions and, indeed, had to authorize all capital expenditure down to very small sums. Harry Pilkington laid great stress on detailed control from the top. In 1951, the finance committee, which he chaired, became the Group finance committee 'to control the provision and allocation of capital resources in the Group', the aim being after the recent spell of heavier capital expenditure, to 'restore in from 5 to 10 years a sufficiently strong cash position for large projects ... to be achieved without recourse to borrowing or outside finance'. As the business grew in scale and scope, however, members of the executive found themselves with so much on their hands that (in the words of Arthur Pilkington who became increasingly concerned about the company's management structure), 'they had no time to do anything properly ... Decisions were delayed.'

8

Restructuring

By 1955 the company was employing 20,000 people, 3,000 of them overseas. It was then decided to devolve responsibility to two management committees, one for flat glass, and the other for pressed glass; and more authority was given to the boards of subsidiary companies. In 1958, four advisory committees were added: Finance, Research and Development, Sales, and Personnel. Although these allowed wider discussion of policy matters, the Group executive did not always heed the advice which came up to them from these committees; and the new arrangements did not ease the directors' burdens, for one or two of them sat on each advisory committee. Individual authority for each capital requisition was still limited to £10,000.

At the end of the 1950s, Harry Pilkington started to issue annual reports to the staff and took the opportunity to introduce each of these at a special meeting held in St Helens. When a fellow director ventured to ask whether he would answer questions after his first speech, he was told, without a moment's hesitation: 'Certainly not!' The Pilkington family knew how to run its business; and the remarkably favourable results showed this. How the family used its money was its own concern.

So matters rested until Pilkington began to bring outside specialists on to the Group executive on a non-executive basis. Its minutes of 11 February 1964 noted that 'this will be the first time that we have had a true outsider on our Board as Director'. This 'true outsider' was Sir Humphrey Mynors who had just completed ten years as Deputy Governor of the Bank of England. Sir Norman Kipping joined him in 1965 at the end of his long tenure as Director-General of the Federation of British Industries. The strong hand of the Pilkington chairman is to be clearly seen in both these appointments.

Another, and much more decisive, step forward took place in 1965 when Arthur Pilkington was able to pursue his interest in company structure further, having replaced Douglas Phelps as chairman of the Group executive. He and Harry Pilkington produced a paper that recommended substantial management reorganization and this was soon implemented. A Group general board replaced the Group executive and the management committees, by then increased in number, became divisional boards, each with chairmen and managing directors personally responsible for each division's operations within objectives laid down by the Group board. Service

The most successful fourth generation, at the last meeting held in the old board room at Grove Street at the end of July 1964.

(LEFT TO RIGHT, FRONT ROW): Arthur C. Pilkington, Douglas V. Phelps, Colonel Guy Pilkington, Sir Harry (later Lord) Pilkington, Geoffrey L. Pilkington, James B. Watt.

(BACK ROW): Dr Lawrence H. A. Pilkington, Sir Alan Hudson Davies, J. Archer Burns, Lord Peter Cozens-Hardy, David F. Pilkington, Sir Humphrey Mynors, J. Fraser-Rigby (company secretary), G. W. T. (Terry) Bird, George McOnie, Alastair Pilkington.

functions, such as accounting, secretarial and public relations, managed by heads of each function, were to provide the services requested by each division. A planning advisory committee concerned itself with long-term planning and a chairman's consultative committee advised on strategy and tactics required to deal with particular situations as they arose. It could be called together at any time by the company chairman – again we see Harry Pilkington's hand – to discuss important ideas, plans or problems with divisional chairmen, managing directors, senior managers or heads of functions. Finally, a group co-ordinating committee, consisting of head of function and managing directors of operating divisions, was set up to make sure that proper use was being made of functions by divisions and to deal with Group matters not important enough to be referred to the Group board itself. Several experienced men such as John Leighton-Boyce (Finance), Dr D. S. Oliver (R&D) and Blake Pinnell (Planning) were recruited from outside the company to take a lead in these new divisions. Two internal promotions, George McOnie and G. W. T. (Terry) Bird, had joined the executive in 1954 and 1960 respectively.

Here indeed was devolution and a greater measure of power sharing. Those who look back on these radical administrative changes may wonder what effect they might have had on company diversification if they had been made a decade earlier.

Management structure was at last appropriate to the company's size, which had outgrown the ability of the family's human resources to manage through a predominantly family executive committee. It was also realized that, in view of the company's continued growth, the family age profile and the high rate of death duties, the time was not far off when shares would have to be offered to the public if the company was to go on growing. Harry Pilkington, who felt particularly responsible for handling this matter, made it clear that the company would never fail to undertake desirable expansion on the grounds of shortage of money. Company borrowing, even in static 1950 pounds sterling, did not rise above £1 million during that decade as we have seen; but after then it rose sharply (to £35 million by 1970/71) even though most of the capital for growth was found from the returns on the float process and from other

ploughed-back profits. So as early as 1960, a year after the announcement of float, Harry Pilkington decided privately that the earliest date at which the business would go public was likely to be round about 1970. He also saw that it would be impossible to postpone the move for long after that in view of the family's growing difficulty in finding the money to buy shares from estates of deceased shareholders and of the known feeling among a few of the living shareholders that they would like to have a wider market in order to obtain a higher price per share than they could when they sold among themselves.

The decision to transform Pilkington into a public company was taken in January 1970 and the prospectus was issued to the public in the following November, despite a long, unofficial strike – the first major stoppage since 1878 – and a general fall in stock market prices during the intervening months.

When Lord Pilkington – Harry Pilkington became a life peer in 1968 – retired as chairman in 1973, he and the other directors, mostly Pilkington family members of the fourth generation, were able to look back upon twenty-four years during which the company had grown at a rate unprecedented in its earlier history. The capital employed had grown from £12.5 million to £206 million, and sales to outside customers from £15.6 million to £177 million. The numbers employed had increased from 15,233 to 31,200, reflecting a vast increase in labour productivity, and, most significantly, of these totals, those employed abroad had increased from a mere 667 to 9,800. The vast change was symbolized by the new headquarters, a twelve-storey office block in pleasant, landscaped surroundings at Ravenhead, St Helens, occupied in 1964, and including a glass museum, open to the public. In recognition of Pilkington's greater com-

In the mid-1960s, with float glass licensing and royalty income starting to flow in and Pilkington's own involvement overseas about to be increased, outside specialists were introduced. John Alfred Stuart Leighton-Boyce (born 1917), brought in from Chartered Bank, became Group treasurer in 1966. He was soon heavily involved in senior management more generally, and became a main board director in 1971. Of the non-executive outside specialists to be recruited, the first was Sir Humphrey Mynors, in 1964, who had just completed 10 years as Deputy Governor of the Bank of England. He was followed, in 1965, by Sir Norman Kipping at the end of his long tenure as Director-General of the Federation of British Industries. E. T. (Ted) Judge, formerly Chairman and Managing Director of Dorman Long (subsequently Reyrolle Parsons) in 1968 became the third non-executive director.

John Leighton-Boyce

These years saw the long-delayed implementation of major devolution in the company's administrative structure, already started in a small way, in 1958. (Arthur Pilkington, who had long advocated it, became chairman of the executive committee in 1965). A Group general board replaced the Group executive and the managing committees became divisional boards, with chairmen and managing directors responsible for each division's operations within objectives laid down by the general board. In this way, non-family senior managers became more actively involved in the taking of major decisions in the years immediately before Pilkington became a public company in 1970.

mitment to science and technology, a large new research and development complex, situated on a green field site at Lathom about ten miles away from St Helens had been opened in 1961.

Despite the reorganization of the business into divisions in the mid-1960s and its subsequent transformation into a public company in 1970, Pilkington still remained very much a family concern for a few years longer. Because of unfavourable stock market conditions, the family parted with only about 10 per cent of its shares initially and the existing directors continued in office. In consequence, when Lord Pilkington retired in 1973, the board still contained relatively few full-time, non-family members.

J. B. Watt's retirement (in 1971) offset the arrival on the executive (in 1962) of Terry Bird. George McOnie, the other very successful works manager, who had joined the executive committee (in 1954), left it in 1968. (Sir) Barrie Heath, the Managing Director of Triplex, came on in 1967; but his presence, in its turn, only offset the departure of another non-family member, (Sir) Alan Hudson Davies, the year before. During Harry Pilkington's chairmanship, only three promotions to the board resulted from the reorganization of the mid-1960s: in 1970 Rowland Stanley (Robey) Roberson, who had been with the company since 1946 and had distinguished himself in works management, becoming managing director of the flat glass division in 1967; Leslie Newton Wall, who, as we have seen, had brought the negotiation of float licences to a fine art in the earlier 1960s and had subsequently become deputy to George McOnie as chairman of the pressed glass division in 1967 and his successor in the following year, joining the main board in 1970; and in 1971 John Leighton-Boyce, a financial specialist at the Chartered Bank who had applied successfully in 1966 for the new position of Group treasurer and had brought a broader financial approach to the company's affairs during the following critical years. The number of outside non-executive directors was increased to three in 1968 when E. T. (Ted) Judge, who had been chairman and managing director of Dorman Long (subsequently of Reyrolle Parsons), joined Sir Humphrey Mynors and Sir Norman Kipping.

By March 1973, when Lord Pilkington delivered his last chairman's report, a fifth-generation member of the family had become a full-time director. This was Antony Richard Pilkington, Arthur Pilkington's son, who had done his National Service with the Coldstream Guards (in which, as we have seen, his father had served as a regular officer) and then read History at Cambridge. He had arrived as a family trainee in 1959, joining the flat glass division in 1967 and becoming its joint managing director in 1972, an unusually swift promotion as a result of the early and quite unexpected death of R. S. Roberson at the age of fifty-three.

By 1973 two significant management changes had occurred which clearly indicated that the days in which the company would continue to be run by the St Helens Pilkingtons were numbered. When, in 1967, the divisional boards had assumed the responsibilities previously undertaken by the executive committee of the general board, Arthur Pilkington, previously chairman of the executive became executive vice-chairman of the main board and Harry Pilkington its chairman. In 1971 Terry Bird replaced Arthur Pilkington as executive vice-chairman and Sir Alastair Pilkington became deputy chairman and Harry Pilkington's heir apparent.

Despite these two clear signs of things to come, Pilkington remained essentially a family business so long as Lord Pilkington was its chairman. Such was his reputation and prestige outside the company as one of Britain's most outstanding businessmen, and within it as the person who more than anyone else made possible its un-precedented growth and achievement, that Harry Pilkington's influence was all pervasive. Nobody knew the flat glass industry better than he, its leading personalities (and often its humble lieutenants, too) in all parts of the world, and its problems. His supreme

SUCCESSFUL WORKS MANAGERS WHO BECAME PILKINGTON DIRECTORS AFTER THE MID-1950s

(LEFT): George McOnie (1903–1988).

George McOnie, another product of Allan Glen's School, Glasgow, and an engineer by training, had joined Pilkington in 1927. He became such an effective time-and-motion specialist in the 1930s that the directors had asked him to go more easily. He later became manager at Doncaster and then at Cowley Hill before joining the executive in 1954 and becoming a full director in 1958.

(RIGHT): George William Terence (Terry) Bird (1914–1985).

Educated at Prescot Grammar School and Imperial College, London, where he read Physics, Terry Bird joined Pilkington in 1935 becoming manager of Sheet Works in 1956, a director in 1962 and vice-chairman of the Group executive from 1971 to 1977.

(LEFT): Rowland Stanley Roberson (Robey) (1918–1972).

R. S. Roberson joined the technical development department, Sheet Works in 1946 and, after spells as works manager at Scarborough, Canada, and Pontypool, South Wales, became general manager, Sheet Works, 1961–1965 and then manager at Cowley Hill. He was managing director of the flat glass division from 1967 and a general board director from 1970. His unexpected death in 1972, aged 53, was a great loss to the company.

Lord Pilkington and his executive directors in 1968.

(LEFT TO RIGHT): Lord Pilkington, Arthur Pilkington, Dr Lawrence Pilkington, Alastair Pilkington, Terry Bird, David Pilkington.

achievement was the presentation of Pilkington's case to the Monopolies Commission in 1965. The conclusion to its report in 1968 must have given him great satisfaction:

We are satisfied that Pilkington is conscious of its responsibility, as a monopolist, to the public interest. This sense of responsibility may be associated to some extent with the long-established dominance of the Pilkington family within the business, reflected, as this still

is [1967], in the status ofPilkington Brothers Limited as a private company ... It is not for us to speculate how long the traditional character of the management of the company may continue, but there would, we think, have to be some quite unforeseen change in this respect before Pilkington would deliberately set out to exploit its position of strength at the expense of the public interest.

Conditions were indeed to change and so was the style of management; but the

personality of the company and its emphasis on long-term objectives rather than short-term gain were to be maintained despite the more difficult economic climate in which it was soon to operate and the fact that the directors no longer owned the business for which they were responsible.

PART THREE

(ABOVE): Sir Alastair Pilkington FRS (1920–)

The very unusual circumstances under which Alastair Pilkington came to St Helens have been explained in Chapter 5, and his invention of and key role in the development of the float process in Chapter 6. For all these services he was elected a Fellow of the Royal Society in 1969 and received a knighthood in the New Year's Honours in 1970. He was awarded many university honorary degrees from various parts of the world and served as Chancellor of the University of Lancaster. He became an honorary Fellow of the University of Manchester Institute of Science and Technology (UMIST) and of both Imperial College, London, and the London School of Economics where he established, and later personally supported financially, a unit for the study and teaching of business history. He was a director of the Bank of England and of BP. A keen musician, he was a member of the management committee of the Royal Liverpool Philharmonic Society. On his retirement from the chairmanship of Pilkington (1973–1980) he became a non-executive member of the board until 1983 and then president of the company in succession to Lord Pilkington, a fitting tribute to his contribution to the company's unprecedented development since the war. In 1993, he was made Chancellor of the University of Liverpool.

9

The Transition:
1973–1980

When Sir Alastair Pilkington became Pilkington's chairman, on 1 September 1973, the company was riding high. Demand for glass was strong from both the building industry and the motor trade. Indeed, throughout the world it was described at the time as 'unprecedented'. Float glass, steadily developed and operated ever more efficiently, had replaced plate glass and was already overtaking the more expensive qualities of sheet. A new float line (CH2 at Cowley Hill) was started in September 1972, with the intention of replacing some of Pilkington's sheet glass output. A year later, along with the company's other float plants, it was working to capacity. Licensing income and technical fees had already contributed £13 million net to pre-tax Group profits of £34 million in the financial year 1972/73 and was forecast to rise during the rest of the decade. (It did, reaching £37 million in 1979/80.) Sir Alastair had the satisfaction of presiding over the company's affairs when the income from his successfully developed invention became of increasing value. The company had splendid plans to make the most of this windfall by reinvesting most of it so as to emerge stronger than ever internationally when float royalties began to peter out later on.

This very favourable economic climate, however, soon turned very stormy. War broke out in the Middle East early in October 1973. Within days the posted price of oil shot up by 66 per cent and very soon the Arab states were contriving to cut output and force the price up very much more. Apart from the resulting national three-day week, this, the beginnings of the first of the two great oil shocks, hit Pilkington in two ways: directly, by increasing the price of oil with which some of its furnaces were heated, and indirectly, by reducing the demand for motor vehicles, a major outlet for glass which also reduced the throughput at its value-adding safety glass plants. Building demand, hardly affected in that financial year, 1973/74, also came to be severely reduced in 1974/75. As Sir Alastair then put it in his annual report: 'While our industry has always experienced cyclical demand, we have just experienced the most rapid plunge from peak to trough that anyone can recall.' (For the glass industry this certainly included the time of the world economic crisis at the beginning of the 1930s.) To make matters worse, government price restraint prevented Pilkington from offsetting its higher costs by putting up glass prices in Britain *pro rata*. The Group's trading profit in 1974/75 dropped to a mere £7 million on issued share capital of £60 million and total assets valued at over £300 million. Net income from licensing and technical fees, £15 million that year, was then to be seen in a rather different light. Some of the investment programme had to be postponed for the time being. Profits fortunately picked up after that; prices also went on rising, at rates far greater than the much-quoted great inflation of the sixteenth century, as Britain approached its even better-remembered 'Winter of Discontent'. Times were certainly changing for Britain. And for Pilkington, too.

Sir Alastair's own distinctive stamp of management served the company well in these rapidly changing circumstances. At a Group conference, held only a couple of months after his becoming chairman, he adopted the critical, analytical approach and belief in wide consultation that had typified his able and careful advocacy during the long (and often difficult) days when the float process was being developed. He told Pilkington's senior managers assembled from all over the world at the Lygon Arms, Broadway, in November 1973 :

> We alone have a collective responsibility to examine ourselves, to understand the meaning of being an international company, to recognise what identity we have in different parts of the world, and to shape the identity of the future in the light of our current strengths and weaknesses. ... Every company has an identity. Slater Walker has a different identity from ICI or the Coal Board. Identities are the conscious or unconscious result of applying a policy ...
>
> Take some of our policies. We had a policy for more than a century that making flat glass of all qualities and thicknesses should be the main part of our business ... A policy that encouraged

manufacture overseas when the time was right. A belief in R&D. A feeling of responsibility towards employees after they became pensioners.

Sir Alastair accepted the fact that Pilkington was a technology-based not a market-based company and admitted that it had 'not been too successful' in new product development. He even doubted whether it could handle a new consumer product and deduced, therefore, that Pilkington policy ought to be that of continued concentration upon flat glass and allied activities.

When he came to make his first report to shareholders some six months later, he listed among the company's strengths a strong balance sheet and a willingness to take account of the changing value of money (a reference to Sir Harry's advocacy of inflation accounting which went back to 1949: it was in fact a logical adaptation of the company's depreciation accounting of 1931). Pilkington's international spread was another great strength: it already manufactured in ten countries and on every continent, 'a spread which', he believed, 'is wide enough to reduce the sensitivity of the whole Group to adverse conditions in some part of it'. This may have been true when he was writing but was to prove less the case in the changed circumstances of the future.

The same may be said about Sir Alastair's belief, also expressed in his first annual report, that depressions in building and the motor trade were essentially short-term affairs that punctuated the normal order of things. For him in those pre-Thatcher years, government price restrictions could be as damaging to the company as trade depressions:

> Both building and the motor trade can be affected by relatively short-term factors

such as Government decisions and the general level of the economy. But, in looking for long-term continuity, we know that houses and motor cars will continue to be built and throughout the world where living standards, of which building and transport are key elements, are steadily rising.

An important point that was not emphasized in the early 1970s, however, was that, while demand was likely to grow, so was the glass industry's ability to meet it and, indeed, to overproduce. The float process, by making it possible for high-quality glass to be manufactured at far lower fixed cost per production unit, encouraged manufacturers to start making glass of plate glass quality in parts of the world much sooner than they would otherwise have dreamed of doing. And, try as they might, the existing association of gentlemanly glassmakers could no longer confine manufacture to their own exclusive membership.

As well as the additional unit at Cowley Hill, Pilkington also started a float line at Dandenong near Melbourne, in February 1974, to replace the existing sheet glass facility in Sydney. It was to start another at Springs in South Africa in April 1977. Much more challenging was its decision to make float glass in Scandinavia, the only developed region in the world as yet uncolonized by the gentlemanly glassmakers.

Pilkington, unlike the continentals, and especially St Gobain, had no interest in glassmaking or even in glass processing anywhere in the Nordic area before the later 1960s. The motor industry in Sweden was then growing quickly, however, at Volvo and Saab. Triplex was keen to get orders. This brought it in contact with Hector & Co. AB of Stockholm, a subsidiary of which, Sunex Sakerhetsglas AB, was a major supplier of toughened safety glass to the Swedish motor industry in competition with Trempex, a national competitor in which St Gobain had an interest. Sunex had plans to replace its existing factory near Stockholm with new works at Lysekil near Gothenburg, closer to the motor industry. It lacked the latest technology, however, which was available to its rival through St Gobain. Harry Hector, the chairman, a retired judge of the Stockholm court, therefore agreed to the British taking a financial stake in Sunex in return for the necessary technical know-how and equipment.

The financial negotiations were complex and this resulted in the involvement of John Leighton-Boyce, Pilkington's recently appointed treasurer. Sunex became a Pilkington subsidiary in 1968. Thereafter, the company supplied all Sunex's raw glass for toughening and Triplex sold it laminated windscreen glass, which it did not manufacture itself. In 1972, Pilkington was also able to acquire a majority interest in the third Swedish safety glass concern, Scanex, which did make laminated glass. The main Finnish laminator, Lamino OY, which enjoyed a large export market, followed in 1973.

The importance of the original Sunex investment became more evident as Pilkington developed its international float glass strategy in Sir Harry's last years as chairman. As float was coming to replace sheet, it was evident that the three sheet glass manufacturers in Scandinavia (Scanglas in Denmark, Emmaboda in Sweden and Drammens in Norway) would be affected; and as the United Kingdom's (and Denmark's) belated entry into the European Economic Community approached – it finally happened on 1 January 1973 – the importance of a float glass manufacturing base in the northern part of Europe, within and without the

The flat glass division board in August 1973.

(LEFT TO RIGHT): Michael Winter, Bill Almond, David Pilkington, Ken Earle, Ray Crosbie (joint managing director), David Platt (secretary – standing), John Leighton-Boyce (chairman), Antony Pilkington (joint managing director), Billy Jones, Denis Cail, Bill Darlington, Jim Brackenridge.

Common Market, became more obvious. What was to be Pilkington's share in it?

John Leighton-Boyce, already concerned, became chairman of Pilkington's flat glass division (which was responsible for the rest of Europe as well as the United Kingdom) in January 1972 and Antony Pilkington, previously flat glass division marketing director, became the division's joint managing director. In 1974 he succeeded John Leighton-Boyce as chairman. He was a strong advocate of a Pilkington-controlled float plant in

Scandinavia and, within a month of his appointment as joint managing director, he produced a memorandum on the subject, warning of the danger of being out-manoeuvred by St Gobain.

Pilkington's negotiations with the Scandinavian sheet glassmakers, on the one hand, and St Gobain, on the other, were tortuous and prolonged. St Gobain claimed control of the proposed Scandinavian float glass venture by virtue of its financial interest in the existing sheet and safety glass concerns there. But

Pilkington held the strongest card: possession of the float glass patents. Both sides carried out feasibility studies. Pilkington made a search for the best site, which it eventually identified as being situated at Halmstad, a port on the Swedish coast about ninety miles south of Gothenburg which also had good communication with Denmark. By November 1973 it had obtained an option on a seventy-three-acre site there. Float Glass AB (eventually renamed Pilkington Floatglas AB) was registered as a wholly-owned Pilkington subsidiary.

St Gobain, for its part, was also making its own efforts to gain supremacy in the struggle to obtain the Scandinavians' support. It paid a high price for further shares in Emmaboda and two Swedish glass merchants. Scanglas, which, though a Danish concern, was 70 per cent owned by Grangesberg, a large Swedish business with more interest in metals than in glass, was a key in the negotiations, but the Swedes were playing hard to get. At the end of January 1974, fearing lest this would cause Pilkington to settle with St Gobain on less than favourable terms, Antony Pilkington drew the board's attention to St Gobain's dominance in float glass throughout Europe. It already had a 27,200-gross-tonnes weekly tank capacity spread over five countries: Pilkington possessed only 12,300 tonnes in Europe, all of it in the United Kingdom. A 4,000-tonne tank in Scandinavia would increase St Gobain's lead even further. Pilkington sales in the area already amounted to the output of half a float tank. It should chance its arm and go it alone. The board decided to do so.

Pilkington began to build its new Scandinavian factory in May 1974. The company did not break off negotiations with St Gobain at once, however, but tried to involve its old rival on Pilkington terms;

but by the end of 1974 the European market for float glass had deteriorated to such an extent that St Gobain, realizing that it already had much excess float glass capacity, withdrew from the venture, leaving Pilkington, advantageously placed financially because of its growing income from float glass licensing, to continue building the factory on its own. After St Gobain's departure, Grangesberg came back into the picture for a time; but when even the modern and efficient Scanglas factory could no longer withstand the greater competition from float, Grangesberg also withdrew (in August 1975). When Halmstad opened later in 1976, therefore, it was as a wholly-owned Pilkington subsidiary.

Higher oil prices, which had disadvantaged Pilkington by raising its fuel costs and, for the the time being, reduced the market for flat glass, did bring the company some compensating advantages. More expensive energy encouraged better insulation of buildings and pipes against heat loss. There was not only a great demand for double glazing but also – and more particularly – for the glass wool products produced by Fibreglass. Capacity was greatly increased and a new factory, opened at Pontyfelin in South Wales in October 1976, absorbed some of the employees from the sheet glassworks at Pontypool, closed the year before. The earlier acquisition, in 1973, of Kitsons Insulations Ltd, thermal insulation contractors, proved very timely. A substantial stake in the insulation division of Bernard Hastie Ltd (renamed Hastie Insulations Ltd) followed in 1976.

Fibreglass also possessed a reinforcements division which, as we have seen, possessed a new and modern plant at Wrexham. Glass fibres had been used to reinforce plastics in the pressing of, for instance, the hulls of small boats. In the late

Pilkington float glass factory at Halmstad, Sweden, a port town 90 miles south of Gothenburg.

From 1968 Pilkington acquired an increasing stake in Sweden's safety glass industry, then sending increasing supplies to the motor factories of Volvo and Saab. Antony Pilkington, then flat glass division's marketing director, became a strong advocate of a Pilkington-controlled float glass plant to supply the Nordic area, and John Leighton-Boyce, chairman of the flat glass board from 1972, who had been much concerned with Pilkington's investment in Swedish safety glass, supported him. In 1972, Antony Pilkington became joint managing director of the flat glass board and in 1974 he succeeded John Leighton-Boyce as its chairman. Pilkington Floatglas AB was registered as a fully-owned Pilkington subsidiary in 1974, Pilkington decided to build at Halmstad and the factory was opened in 1976.

1960s, however, the invention of an alkali-resistant glass fibre by the National Research Development Corporation at the Building Research Establishment made it possible to reinforce cement. Pilkington took an exclusive licence to manufacture and market the product. Important development took place at Pilkington's research and development laboratory at Lathom, and in his second annual report (for 1974/75) Sir Alastair was full of enthusiasm for Cemfil, as the new discovery was called. This enabled not only heavier concrete pipes to be replaced by lighter substitutes, but also high-strength, thin-section, fire-resistant products to be made from cement, a relatively inexpensive material which was used throughout the world. For some purposes, they could replace timber, cast iron and steel. The possibilities seemed enormous, not least the replacement of asbestos, which was causing concern for health reasons. Here indeed was the possibility of a major diversification out of flat glass yet within Pilkington's proclaimed policy of confining itself to 'flat glass and allied activities'. As a new technological development, Cemfil was soon recognized by a Queen's Award to Industry.

Pilkington commissioned a new plant at its Wrexham site to meet the expected demand. It did not intend to rush ahead too fast, however, for the company did not forget 'the disrepute that had once been attached to reinforced plastics because of a failure to control the standards of some early enthusiasts'. To ensure that users were properly instructed in the best use of the new material, the Building Research Establishment and Pilkington produced an Incorporation Licence, whereby industrial companies acquired the two licensors' expertise in the design, manufacture and testing of glass-reinforced cement (GRC) products while Pilkington had the last word in the way in which Cemfil fibres were to be used. By early 1975, more than 200 companies in the United Kingdom and overseas had been licensed, including major international organizations in Germany, Japan, North America, Australia and South Africa. Pilkington had also formed, with Tunnel Cement and Associated Portland Cement, joint subsidiaries to develop specific GRC products and high-volume machinery to make them. Looking even further ahead, Pilkington had initiated research programmes to see if GRC might have load-bearing structural applications.

Pilkington also had a second avenue of diversification which seemed to offer prospects no less glittering, for it might enable it to steal a march on all rivals in safety glass. Laminated windscreens, demanded in North America, were also becoming more popular in Europe, in preference to zone-toughened glass. It was believed that, for safety reasons, the EC Commission would insist on laminated in due course. Pilkington, therefore, instituted research (originally in collaboration with St Gobain and Boussois) to produce a windscreen superior to the existing laminated product – the 'Ideal Windscreen'. It found that two pieces of 2.3 mm float, highly stressed in a new process and with a new interlayer, would reduce by 90 per cent the amount of laceration due to the head's impact with the windscreen. In 1974, Ten Twenty, as it was called, was in its pre-production stage. It was first used in the Rover 3500, a quality car. A new production line, installed at Kings Norton during the 1970s, was considered of sufficient importance to be opened by the Prime Minister, James Callaghan, at the end of August 1978. A second line was commissioned that year.

There was one great snag, however. The new product could not be produced at a price acceptable to the highly competitive and sales-resistant automotive industry. It was more costly to produce than existing laminated windscreens. The initial capital cost was higher and so were operating costs. A higher proportion of glass produced was substandard and had to be rejected; and the cost of changing over to another windscreen size was greater and took longer. The few powerful customers in the motor industry resisted the inevitably higher price asked for this 'Ideal Windscreen', especially as the new asymmetrical laminated windscreens were already safer than the older type. Only the aircraft manufacturers were prepared to buy. Without a large potential market, Pilkington was also unable to find any licensees. A good and very worthy idea did not prove a commercial success.

FURTHER DIVERSIFICATION HOPES OF THE 1970s

(ABOVE): Cemfil.

Pilkington took an exclusive licence from the National Research Development Corporation for an alkali-resistant glass fibre with which it was possible to reinforce cement. Important development was undertaken at Lathom which enabled heavy concrete pipes to be replaced by lighter substitutes and thin section, fire resistant products to be made. By 1975 more than 200 companies had been licensed to make these products.

(RIGHT): Ten Twenty, the 'ideal windscreen' which reduced laceration on impact by 90 per cent.

Conventional laminated

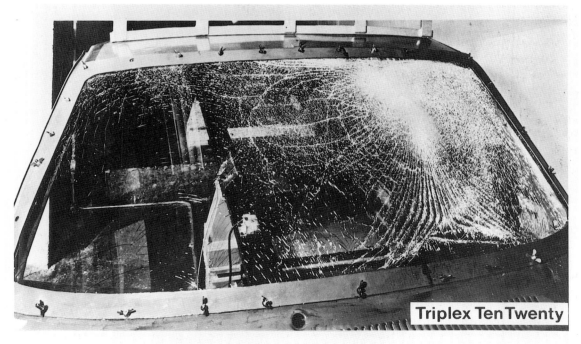

Triplex Ten Twenty

The Pilkington main board in 1976 under the chairmanship of Sir Alastair Pilkington (1973–1980).

With the income from float glass licensing rising, the future looked bright when Sir Alastair Pilkington became chairman in 1973; but the first oil shock reduced the demand for glass, first from the motor industry and then for building, at a time when new float glass lines were coming on stream in various parts of the world. Profits fortunately picked up after 1974/75.

Among other remarkable developments during the decade was Chance–Pilkington Reactolite (1973), later developed further as Reactolite Rapide (1977), marketed in prescription sunglasses and those which darkened and cleared more rapidly than any other photochromic glass. A chemically-toughened version was also developed. Reactolite Rapide came on the market during the financial year 1977/78 and also received a Queen's Award to Industry. St Asaph was also interested in producing optical fibre for communication purposes and in holography. The use of infra-red glasses opened up new prospects for the

defence work there of Pilkington–PE (formerly Pilkington Perkin Elmer), the company's electro-optical subsidiary.

Against the promise of these various developments, especially Cemfil and Ten Twenty, the loss of the television bulb business (another possible route to diversification in the 1950s) seemed less important, although as Sir Alastair later admitted, it was a great blow to the company. Early in 1975, the manufacture of television tubes, in which 5 per cent of Pilkington assets were invested, was reported as 'in serious difficulty' because of increased imports from Japan and higher levels of VAT on television sets. In January of the following year, Thorn Colour Tubes at nearby Skelmersdale closed. Pilkington manufacture of glass bulbs at Ravenhead stopped a month later.

The success of Reactolite boosted Pilkington's ophthalmic activities considerably. The Michael Birch Group, ophthalmic manufacturing opticians and makers of microfilm equipment, acquired in 1974 as we have seen, provided a valuable outlet, though attempts to expand further downstream were stopped when the Monopolies Commission vetoed the purchase of UK Optical. Further significant growth soon occurred in this field, however, when, in February 1979, Pilkington bought for £24 million all the share capital of Sola Holdings Ltd, an Australian-based concern that had become one of the world's leading manufacturers and distributors of plastic prescription lenses for spectacles. Already operating in eight countries, Sola was soon to carry Pilkington much further into the eye-care business as we shall see.

Much of Sir Alastair's last two years as chairman – he retired in September 1980 but remained as a non-executive member of the board – were taken up with negotiations which led to the acquisition of one of the most efficient flat and safety glass concerns in continental Europe, Flachglas AG – the main flat glass manufacturer in West Germany – and the holding company Dahlbusch. This had been acquired a decade earlier by Boussois–Souchon–Neuvesel (BSN) of which Antoine Riboud, one of the most outstanding entrepreneurs of his day, had become president in 1966, having acquired the flat glass company, Glaces de Boussois, and merged it with his family bottlemaking company, Souchon–Neuvesel of Lyon. He horrified the whole gentlemanly glass industry by his attempt to take over the far older and larger giant,

St Gobain, in 1968. The bid failed but, undeterred, he acquired Flachglas AG in 1970 and, two years later, a controlling interest in the Belgian flat glass producer, Glaverbel. In the meantime, realizing (as he later confessed) that 'it would be better to fill bottles than just to make them', he bought a number of mineral water businesses and breweries (including Evian, Kronenbourg and Kanterbrau). In 1973 he merged BSN with France's largest food business, Gervais–Danone, which specialized in cheese, yoghurt, desserts and pasta. He soon came to see that food and drink were more profitable than glassmaking, especially in the difficult 1970s. This was the background against which Sir Alastair was eventually able to acquire for Pilkington a 54.8 per cent share in Flachglas AG and an 81 per cent share in Dahlbusch in June 1980 for £113 million. (Glaverbel went to the Japanese glassmaker, Asahi, in 1981 and Boussois to PPG.)

Flachglas AG had resulted from the merging of two German businesses: Delog (Deutsche Libbey–Owens Gesellschaft, formed in 1925 to exploit the Libbey–Owens flat drawn process) and Detag (Deutsche Tafelglas AG, a joint stock company formed in 1932, at the depth of the world depression) to rescue three older concerns, two of which already operated the Fourcault flat drawn process. Delog's centre of operations was at Gelsenkirchen in the Ruhr and Detag's at Weiden in northern Bavaria, not far from the Czech frontier, though it also controlled a factory at Witten, near Gelsenkirchen, the origin of which, like Pilkington, went back to the 1820s. After the Second World War, Delog and Detag both grew considerably, the former, for instance, adding the PPG window glass process and the latter acquiring a factory at Wernberg-Köblitz, near Weiden, which had been making safety glass since 1938 under the trade name Sigla. Cudo insulating glass and mirrors were soon added. Delog also began to make laminated safety glass and insulating units in the mid-1950s. By the time float glass came on the scene, both were businesses which made and polished thick sheet glass and added much value to their product by further processing. But they were not plate glass manufacturers and as such were not likely to receive a float glass licence from Pilkington.

With Riboud's backing, however, and as part of BSN, Flachglas could claim such a licence. It then proceeded to modernize and rationalize its factories in the Ruhr, in Bavaria, and elsewhere. All its raw glass manufacture was concentrated at three float plants, two of them at Gladbeck in the Ruhr and the third at Weiherhammer near Weiden. The processing plants were extended in both locations. The company no longer made window glass in Austria but produced patterned glass and Profilit, a channel-profiled product used in building, which Pilkington at the time manufactured under licence.

The Flachglas AG deal also had implications for Pilkington in South America where it had given up safety glass processing in Brazil in the mid-1960s. St Gobain had concentrated its activities in Brazil in 1960 after selling its interest in VASA, Argentina, to Pilkington and its other associates, Boussois and Glaverbel. VASA, in its turn, had joined forces in Argentina with the Paris-based grain and general merchants, Louis–Dreyfus et Cie, in their very successful safety glass business, Santa Lucia, located in the suburbs of Buenos Aires. In return, Louis–Dreyfus had acquired a stake in VASA. Pilkington also acquired a 50 per cent share in Blindex at São Paulo, Brazil, which Louis–Dreyfus had launched as well, and in Providro, a new sheet glass factory at

Caçapava in that country in which the Paris concern also had an interest.

In 1980 Pilkington was building a new and much more efficient float plant at St Helens (UK5). This would replace CH1. The original move from plate glass to float had not resulted in any unemployment for Pilkington workers. Those who did not take early retirement on advantageous terms had then been found jobs elsewhere. By the 1970s, however, with more efficient float plants and the closure of the more labour-intensive sheet glass machines, the company was at last confronted with the need for compulsory redundancies.

In meeting this new situation, Pilkington showed an initiative that was later copied by the government itself. Pilkington's annual report for 1977/78 announced the creation of the Community of St Helens Trust Ltd by which it, together with other local business sponsors, trade unions and local government would provide not only the finance but also the necessary specialist advice and management training to enable some of those made unemployed to start businesses of their own in St Helens, and to see them through the most difficult first three to five years. In February 1980 Rainford Venture Capital Ltd, in which Pilkington was joined by BP, the Prudential and NatWest, was also created to support and fund entrepreneurs and to foster employment. By September 1992, 1,351 businesses had been supported, with a remarkable 80 per cent survival rate.

Economies at home and relaxation of the British government's price restraints, together with considerably larger contributions from companies overseas, allowed trading profits to rise slowly from the exceptionally low point of £7.5 million to which they had fallen in 1974/75 to about £50 million. Licensing income and technical fees reached £37 million in 1979/80 as we have seen. From these

The Flachglas AG factory at Weiherhammer near Weiden in northern Bavaria, not far from the Czech frontier, after a second float line had been added in 1990.

During Sir Alastair's chairmanship, Pilkington expanded much more rapidly abroad than at home and even before the acquisition of a major share in Flachglas AG, Germany's largest flat glass manufacturer, in 1980, Pilkington sales in continental Europe were already a third of those in the United Kingdom. Flachglas AG had already undergone much concentration and modernization in the 1970s. Two float lines had been built at Gladbeck in the Ruhr and a third at Weiherhammer. Flachglas AG also possessed up-to-date safety glass and other facilities in both areas which added value to the raw product.

Bill Humphrey, later recognised as the inventor of the enterprise agency, became the first Director of the Community of St Helens Trust, a key organization in fostering job creation in St Helens in which Pilkington plays a continuing part.

In the later 1970s Pilkington, in collaboration with other businesses in the area, trade unions and local authorities (and later with BP, the Prudential and NatWest) formed several organizations to finance new businesses and provide management training and advice in order to foster job creation in the area. This proved important in the more difficult years to come. By 1992, over 1,300 businesses had been supported with an 80 per cent survival rate.

Bill Humphrey

profits, the company in the ten years after it went public managed to reinvest £380 million in modernization of existing plant and new ventures. Financial prudence remained the rule: only £75 million was borrowed during the 1970s, bringing total loan capital and bank overdrafts to £136 million in 1980. A further £62 million was raised in 1979 from shareholders by means of a rights issue.

As he looked back over his seven years as chairman, Sir Alastair confirmed that the company's strengths remained the same as those he had listed in his first report to shareholders, though he added that change had been a major feature since then. 'Because change is now normality,' he noted, 'the companies which will survive are those which will react fast enough.' Swift reactions, however, meant that there might be insufficient attention

paid to longer-term planning – 'that we are so busy reacting that we create nothing. It is of profound importance that companies should not only react well but that they should also devote much energy to the *creation* of the future.'

During his chairmanship, the company had grown faster abroad than at home. By 1980 Pilkington employed 22,600 people in the United Kingdom (12,550 at St Helens) and 12,400 abroad. (In 1973 the totals had been 21,400 and 9,800 respectively.) Sales to outside customers were £629 million in 1979/80 (against £177 million in 1973), 51 per cent in the United Kingdom and 49 per cent abroad. This clearly showed the high level of UK-manning per unit of sales. It is notable, too, that by March 1980 – before the acquisition of Flachglas AG – sales in continental Europe were already a third of those in the United Kingdom. Risks were certainly being spread internationally; and, as has been seen, further precautions had been taken by diversification at home from flat glass into allied activities. Much, however, depended upon the success of these activities. There was already some doubt about Ten Twenty, for the motor industry was reluctant to pay more for laminated windscreens in any but the most expensive models. In any case, the greater use of seat belts in cars seemed to make safer windscreens less necessary. Cemfil continued to make progress but at a slower pace than was originally hoped. Indeed, in the year 1979/80 safety glass and glass fibre reinforcements both made losses, unlike the fibreglass insulation division and Chance-Pilkington with Reactolite. And among Pilkington operations abroad, those in Canada, where a large proportion of its overseas investment was located, were in difficulty – and had been for some time – because of intense competition from the Americans. After a sixteen-week strike at the Pilkington factory at Scarborough, Toronto, the older of Pilkington's two float lines there was not restarted. Despite some undoubted successes, coming events were starting to cast their shadow at home and abroad.

During these years, as family directors were further replaced by senior managers, Pilkington had ceased to be a family business in all but name. In 1975 Denis Cail, who had joined the company in 1947 as a technical assistant and moved up the management ladder on the production side, joined Leslie Wall, John Leighton-Boyce and Sol Kay on the board. Dr Dennis Oliver, head of R&D, and Geoffrey Iley, who had been managing director of Triplex and Australia, came on in the following year. When Terry Bird retired as deputy chairman in September 1977, Leslie Wall and John Leighton-Boyce were promoted as joint deputy chairmen. In 1980, three other Pilkington men with long service,

Denys Cledwyn-Davies, Bill Snowden and Mervyn Windsor, joined the board. On the other hand, the two very influential family members, Lord Pilkington and Arthur Pilkington, ceased to be non-executive directors and left the board altogether.

Sir Arnold France, recently retired as Chairman of the Board of Inland Revenue, became an outside non-executive director in 1973; Sir Leonard Neal, the industrial relations specialist, followed in 1976 (when Sir Humphrey Mynors left) and Lord Croham (Sir Douglas Allen, formerly head of the Home Civil Service) in 1978/79. In that year Ted Judge retired and Antony Pilkington, who had shown such initiative and ability in the Scandinavian venture, succeeded Leslie Wall as joint deputy chairman when the latter retired from full-time directorship. John Leighton-Boyce, the other deputy chairman, retired from that post at the end of 1980. He had been succeeded by Denis Cail as sole deputy chairman in September 1980 when Antony Pilkington replaced Sir Alastair as chairman. Only David Pilkington, the youngest member of the fourth generation, remained with Antony as a full-time family director, and David Pilkington was to retire in October 1985. Originally on the production side of the business, he had latterly been in charge of personnel and also concerned himself increasingly with links between the company and the local community.

By 1980 the non-family presence had become so strong that, as Sir Alastair testified, it had:

almost been made more difficult for him [Antony] to reach this position than would have been the case had he not been a member of the Pilkington family. He has had to establish himself at every level in the company and has proved to his colleagues that he is the right person to take on the job.

David Frost Pilkington, the last board member of the fourth generation, joined the company on the production side in 1947 after an engineering degree at Cambridge and service in the RNVR. He joined the board in 1959 and in 1970 became director in charge of Personnel. He retired in October 1985.

David Frost Pilkington (1925–)

Antony Pilkington was a large shareholder; but by then the family, which had initially parted with only 10 per cent of its shares when Pilkington became a public company, is said to have owned fewer than 15 per cent of them. The years between 1973 and 1980 had seen a complete change from family ownership as well as from family management.

10

Challenge and Development at Home and Abroad

Antony Pilkington was forty-five years old when he became chairman in September 1980, Harry Pilkington's age to a year when he had reached that position just over thirty years before. Like him, Antony had also spent about twenty years with the company, first as a family trainee learning about the business in the works and offices, being reported upon by departmental heads, before being given an increasing amount of managerial responsibility, and eventually, having satisfied all concerned, reaching board level. There, however, the similarity between the two careers ends. Antony Pilkington came to the helm at a very unusual time in British history when the country suffered two deep recessions within not much more than a decade. He and his board, no longer protected by family ownership, also had to withstand an unexpected and unwelcome takeover bid as it was recovering from the first of these. The knighthood he was to receive in 1990 for his services to UK business was no formal honour.

The economic medicine prescribed by the Thatcher Government at the beginning of the 1980s to bring inflation rates back to single figures was far more purgative in its effects than the price restraint and control imposed earlier by the Heath and Wilson administrations in and after 1973.

High interest rates reduced building activity sharply at a time when an overvalued pound – the effects of OPEC's price rise of 1979 upon Britain, then a major oil exporter – made it more difficult for British manufacturers to export and easier for their rivals to sell in Britain. Pilkington's share of its home market fell from over 70 per cent to 50 per cent. Sales of cars were also hit by the high interest rates. The motor industry's demand for glass, already weak, grew weaker. In July 1980, manufacture of Ten Twenty safety glass, a premium product on which the company had pinned such high hopes not so long before, had to be suspended. In March 1981, at the end of his first financial year as chairman, Antony Pilkington had to report a year's loss on UK operations for the first time since the burst of the boom after the First World War sixty years before.

To make matters worse, competition from American manufacturers in Pilkington's long-established Canadian market, which had been worrying and loss-making for some time, now became intolerable. Pilkington had missed an opportunity to gain control of Canadian Duplate, the safety glass outlet, in 1947. This passed to Pittsburgh Plate Glass. Canadian sales outlets were also increasingly controlled by the Americans, who benefited by paying lower duties on glass imported into Canada than Canadian glass paid when sent into the United States. Unable to sustain endless losses Pilkington sold 51 per cent of its Canadian operations to the Ford Motor Company. Well might the Pilkington report for the financial year 1980/81 refer to an 'accumulation of adversity'.

Losses of £12 million from its UK companies, which still accounted for over 40 per cent of Group sales, called for urgent remedial action. Fortunately, the international spread of the business provided the necessary insurance: profits from abroad made this remedial action possible and float royalties from foreign licensees remained high. Companies outside the United Kingdom, including the newly acquired Flachglas AG for part of that very difficult year, turned in profits of over £60 million, to which royalties and technical fees added another £35 million. These welcome proceeds enabled the board to embark upon an accelerated investment programme to cut costs. This resulted in a drastic reduction in manpower, the numbers of wage and salary earners employed at St Helens being reduced from 11,500 in 1980/81 to 6,700 in 1985/86. Natural wastage and slightly earlier retirement could not achieve labour economies on such a scale quickly enough. Very large sums were required to persuade employees to take redundancy – well over £90 million. The forward-looking employment-creating activities of the Community of St Helens Trust, the first enterprise agency in the country, proved most timely and helpful. By 1987 more than 500 new businesses had been created with the Trust's managerial help since its inception nine years before.

It was not until 1983/84 that Pilkington's UK companies again returned a small profit even before redundancy charges were taken into account, and not until 1987 that the company's annual report could confidently claim that 'the difficult years of the early 1980s' were definitely a thing of the past. The UK companies made a clear profit of £63 million in 1986/87 and those abroad which had grown in number and importance as we shall see, £166.1 million.

These difficult years also saw very important structural changes in the Group, the logical conclusion to its international growth and increasing complexity since divisionalization had been brought in twenty years before by Antony's father, Arthur, and Harry Pilkington. By the early 1980s Pilkington had 100 subsidiary and related companies (the former more than 50 per cent owned and the latter between 20 and 50 per cent) in the United Kingdom alone, and over 300 other companies all told, scattered across thirty-six countries throughout the world. Further de-centralization was needed to encourage more regional and local initiative. In 1984/85 the board made the chief executives of the various divisions responsible for their operations and profits. Much of the central committee structure was then dismantled. With decision-taking at operational level and wage bargaining carried out at individual sites, the board itself, reduced in number from eleven to seven full-time members, together with its five non-executive directors, was able to concentrate upon overall financial control and longer-term strategy.

Board membership also underwent considerable change at this time. Bill Snowden, the director responsible for Fibreglass Insulation and Reinforcements since 1979, retired in May 1985, followed by David Pilkington and Mervyn Windsor in October and John Leighton-Boyce in

The Pilkington board, with fewer executive and more non-executive directors,
in April 1987.

(LEFT TO RIGHT):
(Seated): Denis Cail (deputy chairman up to 1987), *Lord Croham (formerly Head of the Home Civil Service), Sir Antony Pilkington (chairman).

(Standing): Derek Cook (who became deputy chairman later in 1987), Denys Cledwyn-Davies, *Roger Hurn (Chief Executive, Smiths Industries), Geoffrey Iley, Sir Robin Nicholson, *Sir Peter Thompson (Executive Chairman, National Freight Consortium), Peter Grunwell, *Hilmar Kopper (Chairman, Deutsche Bank).

*Non-executive members

December (Peter Grunwell, Mervyn Windsor's successor in charge of Finance, took Mervyn Windsor's place as full-time director). Roger Hurn, chief executive of Smiths Industries, had become a non-executive director in 1983, and Sir Peter Thompson, executive chairman of the National Freight Consortium, became a non-executive director in the following year. Sir Alastair Pilkington, in recognition of his outstanding contribution to the company, then became company President, a position previously held by Lord Pilkington who had died on 22 December 1983. Sir Robin Nicholson joined the board as an executive director on 1 May 1986. After a distinguished career in the academic world in Britain and in business

Antony, the son of Arthur Pilkington and chairman of the company from 1980, became the last member of the family on the board after the retirement of David Pilkington in December 1985 and was subsequently knighted in 1990. During Sir Antony's chairmanship the company suffered particularly from the effects of two deep depressions, in the early 1980s and in the early 1990s, (the latter being more severe than the former because it was worldwide) and an attempted takeover. Strict economy was enforced in order to cut costs, especially at St Helens where the number of salary and wage earners was cut from 11,500 in 1980/81 to 6,700 in 1985/86. By 1990 it had been cut further, to 5,600. Growth abroad, however, continued unchecked. Although severe American competition in Canada obliged Pilkington to give up the uneven struggle and to part with control of its Canadian operations to the Ford Motor Company in 1980/81, the company returned to north America on a much larger scale in 1982/83 by acquiring a 30 per cent stake in Libbey–Owens–Ford (LOF), exchanged in 1986 for the whole of its glassmaking function. It thus became the second largest manufacturer of flat glass in that huge market. Pilkington companies also built new float glass plants in the Nordic area, and in Germany, as well as at St Helens and in other parts of the world. By 1988 it either owned or had a major stake in six of the seven float lines in the southern hemisphere. Its revolutionary new glassmaking process, having driven out polished plate glass, was further developed to the point at which it also replaced sheet glass manufacture. In 1992 the headquarters of its European flat and safety glass divisional companies were moved to Brussels. Less than a fifth of the operations of the world's largest flat glass manufacturer were then located in the United Kingdom.

Sir Antony Pilkington, Chairman of Pilkington plc, since 1980.

The Chance works at Spon Lane, Smethwick, in the middle of the twentieth century.
Various departments were gradually closed and the whole works shut in 1981.

on the European continent, he had latterly served as Chief Scientist at the Cabinet Office. Sol Kay retired in July and Dennis Oliver in September that year.

The bold decision, taken at the beginning of the 1980s, to return the UK companies to profitability by accelerating investment and thereby cutting costs, resulted in the rapid, final switch from sheet to float glass. The new, larger and more up-to-date float line (UK5), costing £75 million, was started at St Helens on 13 March 1981. The previous September had

seen the closure of the last sheet glass machines in the country, and in June 1981 the rolled plate glass factory at Spon Lane, Smethwick, formerly the headquarters of Pilkington's old rival, Chance Brothers, was closed altogether. In the following year, the Pilkington rolled plate factory at St Helens underwent a complete re-organization.

Pilkington also returned to North America in a way that more than offset its loss of control in Canada. In 1982/83, it was able to acquire for £66 million Gulf &

Western's stake – 30 per cent – in Libbey–Owens–Ford (LOF), the second largest flat and safety glass manufacturer in the United States. As part of the transaction, and in order to satisfy the United States' regulatory authorities, Pilkington relinquished the remaining interest in its Canadian business to the Ford Motor Company and agreed to regard its 35 per cent holding in Vitro Plan SA of Mexico as a trade investment only with no board representation. LOF had diversified into fluid systems and laminated and moulded plastics as well as flat glass. In April 1986, Pilkington acquired 100 per cent of the glassmaking division in exchange for its 30 per cent of the whole. This left LOF free to concentrate on its non-glassmaking interests under the new name Trinova, while Pilkington invested very large sums in upgrading glass manufacture. Pilkington could now claim to be the world's largest producer of flat and safety glass.

The return to profitability in the United Kingdom and the strengthening of the Group worldwide came just in time to allow Pilkington to repel a hostile takeover bid launched by BTR on 20 November 1986. It was seen off after a contest lasting sixty-three days, in the course of which Pilkington had the considerable satisfaction of securing the wholehearted support not only of its employees, all three main political parties and the media, but also of the previously militantly left-wing St Helens Town Council, with which the company had previously experienced some rather strained relations. When the chips were down, those who appreciated the fundamental strength of the Pilkington Group and its management rallied impressively to its support; and those who still knew little or nothing of the business and its worldwide role suddenly became aware of its existence and national

importance. The cost of its defence against BTR (£9.5 million) had been worth at least that sum in the extensive publicity received by the company.

The need to reduce the effects of cyclical demand on the highly capitalized flat glass industry and to achieve a more predictable stream of profits, led to an intensified search for allied activities. As the decade proceeded, eye care seemed to provide the answer. In the developed parts of the world (and to a certain extent in the still developing parts), the failing eyesight of growing, ageing populations, with larger disposable incomes, ensured more customers not only for spectacles made of glass, but also for plastic spectacles and contact lenses. This was an allied activity that had originally come to Pilkington through Chance, and had been taken a stride further when the Chance–Pilkington Optical Works, opened at St Asaph in North Wales in 1957, had started to produce ophthalmic spectacle blanks on a large scale for the trade. Sola, the Australian-based plastic lens business acquired in 1979, grew impressively as a member of the Group and by 1984, manufacturing in eight countries, was marketing its products throughout the world. In that year, 900 tonnes of optical and ophthalmic glass were exported by the Group to Japan for the resourceful Japanese to process further and sell in their cameras, binoculars, scientific instruments and photocopiers. In the following year Pilkington was able to claim that about 20 per cent of all the lenses in the western world originated in its Ophthalmic division. Reactolite Rapide, the photochromic ophthalmic glass was also doing well and had won another Queen's Award. In December 1985 Pilkington entered the contact lens business by the acquisition (for £42 million) of the US Syntex Corporation. The time was

(ABOVE AND BELOW): The Chance–Pilkington Optical Works at St Asaph had produced spectacle blanks on a large scale since 1957. Sola, the Australian-based plastic spectacle lens business, acquired by Pilkington in 1979, grew impressively and by 1984 was manufacturing in eight countries and selling its products throughout the world. In December 1985, Sola was brought into contact lenses by the acquisition of the US Syntex Corporation. The Sola spectacle business was sold in 1993.

evidently right for Pilkington to move much more decisively into this promising eye-care market.

This it did in 1987 when it bought, for £368 million, Revlon's two vision care businesses: Barnes–Hind, which made and marketed contact lenses, contact lens solutions and spectacle lenses, and Coburn Optical Industries, leading suppliers of ophthalmic lens-processing equipment and accessories to the ophthalmic manufacturing industry. The market was then buoyant enough – and Pilkington was then once more financially strong enough – to offer over 91 million new 50p shares at 290p each to cover 70 per cent of this purchase. The offer document noted that Barnes–Hind and Coburn 'have significant market shares in their products in the United States, which itself represents about half of the world's market for many ophthalmic products ... The addition of the vision care businesses will transform our growing and successful ophthalmic business into one of the world's leaders in the industry.' In fact, about 80 per cent of vision care's sales were in the United States where the two companies were among the leaders in their high-tech industry. Paragon Optical of Mesa, Arizona, was added in 1988. The Ophthalmic division was then rechristened Pilkington Visioncare. The renamed company, and Sir Robin Nicholson, the director immediately responsible for its operations, set to with a will to bring its various parts together and to weld them into a well co-ordinated business. Sola's headquarters were moved from Adelaide to the Barnes–Hind site in Menlo Park, California, and the rationalization of the various operations was set in train. The Group had high hopes for Visioncare's future as part of its plan to expand its advanced technology areas. The aim was for these to represent 30 per cent of the whole undertaking by 1995. 'With

Barnes –Hind and Coburn Optical added to our existing businesses', Antony Pilkington declared in 1988, 'we are already more than half way to the target.'

Whatever longer-term plans the board may have had for Visioncare itself, however, it was still only a very small part of the whole Group. In the financial year ended March 1988, for instance, it contributed a trading profit of only £14 million to the Group's total operating profit of £306 million, though in the following financial year rationalization had more than doubled this contribution to £35 million in a total Group operating profit of £349 million. The core of the business still remained overwhelmingly flat glass and safety glass, which produced trading profits of £239 million and £286 million respectively in those two years. Here too, however, Pilkington had also made great headway. During the previous ten years, the energy needed to produce a tonne of float glass had been reduced by 30 per cent and the life of a float tank had been doubled. The company was also adding value to the raw glass it produced. The sale of double glazed units continued to be strongly promoted. Pilkington's research centre at Lathom also devoted much effort to the investigation of various coatings upon glass. Much work was done on the reflection and transmission characteristics of these coatings over a wide range of wavelengths. When Kappafloat, an off-line vacuum coated product, was announced in 1985, it was described as a low emissivity glass which imparted triple glazing qualities to double glazing in cold climates. Its successor, Pilkington K Glass, was subsequently produced in quantity directly on the float line, another major advance for the float process and for Pilkington technology.

The fibreglass insulation division continued to market its glass wool and

An early advertisement for Pilkington K Glass.

In the 1980s Pilkington concentrated not only on expounding the merits of double glazing to reduce heat loss and save energy, but also upon adding value to its float glass by coatings which improved the efficiency of double glazing. Pilkington K Glass, produced on the float glass line, gives triple glazing performance to double glazing.

other products, though with greater difficulty when the government withdrew its financial help for this important form of energy saving in the home. A major new insulation plant, opened at St Helens in the early 1980s, replaced two older and less efficient ones. A rock fibre manufacturing business and Kooltherm Insulation Products Ltd, a plastic foam business for low-temperature insulation, were acquired in January 1985 and January 1986 respectively. The Kitson Insulation businesses, already owned by Pilkington, CIS Holdings Ltd, the Leicester-based replacement window company, bought in 1983 for £5.5 million and Keith Young (Insulation) Ltd acquired in 1988, all helped to promote Pilkington's energy-saving activities. By 1988 it could claim to produce more home insulation products than all other British insulation manufacturers put together. Nevertheless, even in a profitable year for insulation in the later 1980s, it contributed little more than £20 million profit to the Group's total, less than one-tenth of the profit on flat and safety glass.

After the acquisition of the glassmaking part of LOF in 1986, Pilkington's flat and safety glass division started to report its sales and trading profits for three geographical areas: Europe, North America, and the Rest of the World (mainly South America, South Africa and Australia). Trading profit in relation to turnover in these core parts of the business

*Pilkington's electro-optical division (later named Optronics) made defence equipment.
The Kite night sight was made at St Asaph.*

*The Thermal Observation Gunnery System (TOGS) made by Barr & Stroud, a
Pilkington company in Glasgow.*

were always higher in the later 1980s in the Rest of the World (£73 million on £323 million in 1987/88, for instance) than in North America (£25 million on £421 million in that financial year, far below the 30 per cent contribution from North America to which the chairman had looked forward in the summer of 1986). Europe fell between the two while still providing by far the largest trading profit and turnover (£141 million and £1,082 million respectively).

The other divisions in 1986/87 were insulation (glass and mineral fibres – later called Insulation and Reinforcement), ophthalmic and special glass (later Visioncare and Pilkington Special Glass), electro-optical (defence – later Optronics), and an assortment of smaller ventures which in due course came to report for a few years as Other Trading Companies. These included the former Aircraft and Special Products division, not only the Triplex activities in this field but also the Californian concern Swedlow Inc., acquired in December 1986 for $40.5 million. Pilkington Properties was another of these smaller businesses. It had originally been formed to develop the company's disused sites but branched out further during the property boom of the 1980s. A New Business division was created in 1988/89 'to provide significant new businesses' for Pilkington over the next decade. It started with twelve companies, including Pilkington Communications Systems Ltd and Pilkington Micronics, which produced ultra-thin glass for storage discs, and Pilkington Micro Electronics Ltd. Pilkington and BOC had also each put £8 million into a joint venture, Living Technology, in January 1988 to exploit medical laser technology. Further emphasis on the encouragement of high-tech ventures is clearly to be seen in all these activities.

The higher returns on its flat and safety glass in the southern hemisphere encouraged Pilkington to build, in collaboration with St Gobain, two float plants in Brazil (at Jacerei opened in November 1982 and at Caçapava started in November 1989), and a third, in Argentina at the VASA site, Llavallol, outside Buenos Aires, in February 1989. (St Gobain had by then re-acquired a 40 per cent holding in VASA.) A second float line was also started in Australia at Ingleburn, Sydney, in November 1988. Pilkington then had either full control of, or a major stake in, six of the seven float plants in the southern hemisphere. The last of the sheet glass operations – already international curiosities – in those southern parts of the world were then closed: Providro at Caçapava, in August 1988, VASA, Llavallol, in September 1988 and Whangarei, New Zealand, in February 1991. (Pilkington had acquired the remaining 50 per cent share of Pilkington ACI for £103 million in April 1988 and the ACI share in New Zealand Window Glass, owners of the Whangarei factory in Australia, the following month for £2.5 million. After its closure, New Zealand was supplied with float glass from Australia). Important sales outlets were acquired in Australia by the purchase of Oliver Davey and T&K, and in New Zealand (Winstone Glass).

Pilkington gained other interests in the Pacific area through Nippon Sheet Glass (NSG). Despite its obsolescent-sounding title, NSG had been the second major Japanese glass manufacturer, after Asahi, to be granted a float glass licence by Pilkington, in November 1966. Further contact between Pilkington and NSG, however, came not directly but via LOF which had at one time owned shares in NSG and had been associated with the Japanese company in L–N Safety Glass in

Mexico from 1975. Ten years later, in 1985, NSG and LOF joined Hankuk Glass Industry of South Korea to process safety glass for the growing motor industry there. Pilkingon inherited LOF's stake and, in 1988, repeated the exercise with NSG and Taiwan Glass Industry Corporation in that country. In March 1989 relations between NSG and the Pilkington Group became significantly closer when Pilkington, at that time in need of reducing its high rate of borrowing – net gearing had increased from 39 to 59 per cent of shareholders' funds – agreed to sell a 20 per cent stake in LOF to NSG for £137 million.

Investment continued at a high level in Europe as well as in Australasia and elsewhere in the later 1980s. OY Lahden Lasitehdas (Lahti) started the second float plant in the Nordic area, in Finland, in October 1987 and Pilkington, which then had a minority 44 per cent interest in Lahti, increased this in the following July to 71 per cent. In October 1990 Flachglas AG started a second line at Weiherhammer, well located for sales to the soon to be united Germany and elsewhere in eastern Europe. A fourth line at St Helens (UK6), originally intended to come on stream in 1990, was started up on 2 April 1992.

The delay was caused by the onset of the second recession within the decade, more serious for Pilkington than the first for it was worldwide in its effects and not concentrated, as the first had been, in the United Kingdom and to a lesser extent in the northern hemisphere. Group turnover and operating profit, which had been growing steadily from 1986/87, began to slow down in 1989/90. (Group operating profits in the four financial years concerned were £262 million, £306 million, £349 million and £360 million.) Because of the higher borrowing and interest rates, pre-tax profit actually fell in the last of these years, from £325 million to £314 million.

In the United Kingdom, safety glass orders from the hard-pressed British motor industry were relatively unremunerative and the Treasury's short-term inflationary measures in response to the stock market collapse on Black Monday in October 1987 were ill-judged. House prices rose sharply and the subsequent interest rate rises, needed to squeeze out this consequent price inflation, led to a deeper and more protracted recession than would otherwise have occurred. The UK building industry soon suffered and so did Pilkington. Greater competitiveness in securing a smaller number of defence contracts, also hit Pilkington's Optronics division and affected its UK profits. Operating profits of all Pilkington's UK companies fell slowly but steadily, from £84 million in 1987/88 to £74 million, on a somewhat higher turnover, in 1989/90.

Profits from Europe, excluding the United Kingdom, held up well and even increased a little, from £84 million to £96 million, largely due to better economic management of the German economy by the Bundesbank and the excellent performance of Flachglas AG. Investment in the new float plants in South America and Australia vastly increased output in the Rest of the World. Sales between 1987/88 and 1989/90, grew from £363 million to £602 million. Operating profits, not surprisingly, also grew, from £75 million to £117 million, despite the onset there of economic difficulties. Pilkington's North American businesses, however, despite the Group's heavy investment, were even less profitable than those in the United Kingdom. Operating profits of £38 million on a turnover of £582 million in 1987/88, rose to £62 million on a much larger turnover, £775 million, in 1988/89, but then fell back to a mere £33 million on a slightly higher turnover, £792 million.

The board, which in 1990 was confronted with the daunting prospect of a rapidly deteriorating market for flat and safety glass throughout the world, had undergone considerable change since 1986. It had been reduced to six executive members (chairman, deputy chairman and four others) in 1987 when Denis Cail and Denys Cledwyn-Davies retired. Glen Nightingale, previously chief executive of Pilkington Glass Ltd, then joined the board as director responsible for flat and safety glass in Europe and North America. Derek Cook succeeded Denis Cail as deputy chairman in August 1987 and became group managing director, a newly created position, in 1990. Andrew Robb, then in his mid-forties, finance director of P&O, left that company to take up the same position with Pilkington in December 1989. His predecessor as Pilkington finance director, Peter Grunwell, succeeded Geoffrey Iley, who retired in 1990, as director responsible for flat and safety glass outside Europe and North America.

The next two financial years, 1990/91 and 1991/92, saw profits collapse throughout the world. Between April 1990 and September 1991 basic float prices fell by about 25 per cent in Europe and the United States and by as much as 38 per cent in Australia. Turnover fell little in Europe, more (about one-tenth) in North America and most (about one-third) in the Rest of the World. Group operating profits on flat and safety glass dropped from £293 million in the year ended 31 March 1990 to £139 million two years later. Of this reduction of £154 million, Europe accounted for £94 million, North America – already providing a derisory return on capital in 1989/90 – £17 million and the Rest of the World £43 million. All the Group's other operations added only £67 million to the £293 million profit on flat and safety glass in 1989–90 and £44 million to the £139 million two years later. Most of the £44

million was accounted for by licensing income (£22.6 million) and Visioncare (£21.5 million). 'Market conditions in the flat and safety glass industry during what has become the longest recession since the Second World War', commented Sir Antony in his report for the year, 'have been the worst anyone can remember.'

Confronted by such an unprecedented situation, the board, faced with rapidly deteriorating profits, set about another round of cost cuttings and, where appropriate, selling parts of the business that were absolutely, or relatively, unremunerative or were likely to become so. This process began early in 1990 when the approaching economic blizzard was already in sight. All Pilkington's interests in Cemfil alkali-resistant fibre – another great hope, like Ten Twenty, a few years earlier – and the marketing businesses connected with it were sold to St Gobain. Rubber Reinforcement was divested to NSG. More surprisingly perhaps, the Group also divested itself of the contracting businesses in the former insulation division, Kitsons and Keith Young, the latter having been acquired only a few years before. Half of Pilkington's interest in Optronics, also much less profitable because of the ending of the Cold War, was sold to the French company Thomson–CSF. This gave electronics expertise to that company and widened the customer base in Europe.

Visioncare, as we have just seen, was the main contributor to Pilkington's 'Allied Activities' profits in 1991/92; but even here the Group had experienced disappointments. Visioncare profits had fallen from £35 million in 1988/89 to £25 million in 1989/90 and to a mere £9.6 million in 1990/91 because of what were then described as 'continued problems in the contact lenses and solutions market in the United States'. The management was changed and Coburn Optical, the optical

Removal of eyesores created by local industry during the past two centuries ...

... have resulted in places like Greenbank in St Helens being completely transformed.

he industries responsible for the growth of St elens – coal, glass and chemicals – were also esponsible for dumping their refuse in large, nsightly spoil tips, sand lodges and heaps of emical waste in parts of a district which, not long efore, had been grazing land. During the present entury the chemical industry moved elsewhere and almining ceased. Despite the increasing amount of xhaust gases from motor vehicles, the atmosphere as become less polluted, especially after St Helens ecame a smokeless zone. But the tips of unsightly aste remained, blots on a derelict landscape.

By the early 1990s these were in process of being emoved. Ravenhead Renaissance Ltd, a consortium f industrial landowners and St Helens Metropolitan orough, was formed in March 1988 to attract new vestment to St Helens and to stimulate economic tivity on 230 acres of land immediately to the south nd south west of the town centre. Pilkington roperties was particularly involved. On 50 acres of reenbank, a vast hole, 125 feet deep was excavated, e great depth being explained by the need to win nworked coal there to help finance the whole enture. It fetched £1.5 million. An unprecedently rge government city grant contributed a further £6.3 illion towards removing industrial eyesores from an ea that had by then grown to 500 acres. Much of the oxious waste was buried in an engineered clay-lined offer on the edge of the reclamation site. At reenbank the land was consolidated and prepared or subsequent house building. Nearer to the town entre, on former glassworks land by the canal, a upermarket and hotel were built. From a point earby, a new road was driven to provide quick ccess to the M62 motorway and to sites laid out for rther business development.

Damage to the local landscape in earlier times, for hich all the coal, glass and chemical manufacturers nd especially the latter) bore responsibility, was at st being repaired by the combined efforts of usiness and the municipality aided by financial pport from central government. The area is now ecoming more attractive to newcomers who will reate job opportunities in a much more pleasant nvironment.

machinery business, was sold. Visioncare profits then recovered to £21.5 million in the following year though contact lenses and solutions continued to suffer from poor markets and very disappointing profitability.

During the financial year 1991/92 the company took two major decisions: to form a Flat and Safety Glass Europe division, the headquarters of which was established in Brussels, and to sell its 48 per cent holding in its subsidiary Glass (South Africa) to its partner there, Plate Glass and Shatterprufe Industries for 525 million rands (about £93 million). With the removal of the most important divisional headquarters from St Helens also went the devolution of many of the support services from St Helens to the operating divisions, the logical consequence of the decentralization decision reached nearly a decade before.

In all, proceeds of disposals in 1991–92, apart from the South African sale, totalled more than £120 million. On the other side of the scale, however, was the cost of business reconstruction (£23 million) and losses on the sale of other businesses, notably a German plastics concern, and a further loss (of no less than £13.9 million) incurred by Flachglas AG when the main United States customer for its solar reflectors went bankrupt.

Despite disappointing results and the continued uncertainty about how long the recession would continue, there are good reasons to expect recovery as soon as demand picks up again and profit margins are restored. Flat and safety glass will still be needed for buildings and transport in all the countries where Pilkington retains a dominant position. This position is in part due to the leadership the company retains in research and development.

Pilkington's main research headquarters are at Lathom, with development centres in Germany and the United States. New products, such as the on-line low emissivity K Glass, EZ-KOOL – the solar control automotive glass – and float glass of less than 1 mm thickness for computer discs and liquid crystal displays, are examples of recent successes. In March 1992 Pilkington announced a major development in glass melting: a production-scale all-electric melter which matched or exceeded standards achieved in the manufacture of float glass by existing oil- or gas-fired furnaces and at much lower fixed capital cost.

Sir Antony's chairmanship had seen a great change in Pilkington's geographical spread despite – or indeed spurred on by – the two economic recessions. In 1980, when he became chairman, the business was still very dependent upon activities in the United Kingdom and Europe and upon the proceeds from float royalties: 70 per cent of its operating profit then came from these two sources. Ten years later, on the eve of the second and more severe setback, about half Pilkington profits came from Europe including the United Kingdom (only 20 per cent from the United Kingdom), 9 per cent from the United States and 32 per cent from the Rest of the World. Royalties had by then fallen to £25 –£30 million, 8 per cent of the Group's total profit. Flat glass still accounted for about half of Pilkington's turnover, as it had done in 1980. The share of safety glass had risen from 18 to 27 per cent.

This better international balance is also evident from the location of Pilkington's employees. In March 1980, in a total of just over 35,000, 22,600 worked in the United Kingdom (12,500 of them in St Helens) and 12,400 abroad. The acquisition of Flachglas AG that summer added 6,000 abroad and companies purchased in South America added another 1,000 at a time when the St Helens labour-force, already starting to be reduced, stood at 11,500. 1981 was a milestone year when, for the first time, half the Group's workforce of 40,300 was employed outside the United Kingdom. The trend away from the United Kingdom continued. By 1990 the labour force there had been reduced to 13,650 (only 5,600 at St Helens) and numbers abroad had grown to 46,900 (14,400 of them on the continent of Europe and 14, 300 in North America).

After this, the second recession reduced the total numbers worldwide still further, from 60,550 to 41,058 by 1993. Of these, 7,427 worked in the United Kingdom and 33,631 in the rest of the world.

Sir Antony's chairmanship had also been marked in the earlier 1980s, as we have seen, by significant management changes as more authority was passed from the board to the operating companies. By 1992 not only the number but also the average age of the executive directors was lower than it had been twelve years before. Significantly perhaps, when Derek Cook retired as Group managing director and deputy chairman in June 1992, he was succeeded, as group chief executive, not group managing director, by someone from outside, completely new to Pilkington, whose experience included that of managing companies in the two geographical regions – continental Europe and North America – that had become of particular importance to Pilkington during the previous twelve years. When appointed to the post, Roger Leverton, aged fifty-three, a chartered accountant by training, was President and Chief Executive of Indal, a subsidiary of RTZ based in Canada with operating companies throughout Canada and the United States which supplied North America's building and automotive industries.

Since the Second World War, Pilkington has changed, very reluctantly at first but then at an ever increasing rate, from a UK manufacturer and exporter of flat and

Roger Leverton (born 1940) was completely new to Pilkington when he was appointed Group chief executive in July 1992. Prior to joining Pilkington, he was president and chief executive of Indal, a subsidiary of RTZ plc, operating in North America, one of the regions of particular interest to Pilkington over the last decade.

Roger Leverton

safety glass into a vast international business, manufacturing first in the British Commonwealth and Argentina and then elsewhere in Europe and in the United States. The important move into the Nordic countries and the decision to acquire a majority holding in Flachglas AG had been made during Sir Alastair's chairmanship in the 1970s. Their considerable effects upon the Pilkington business first became evident in and after 1980 when Sir Antony had taken over. In his time the pace of acquisition abroad has accelerated. The Pilkington board has added the United States, the wealthiest economy in the world, to its major spheres of influence. In 1993 Pilkington remains a British company, British owned, with its Group headquarters remaining at St Helens; but less than one-fifth of its world wide business remains in the United Kingdom.

Contemporaries are always preoccupied by present and recent events: in Pilkington's case by the effects upon the business of world-wide economic recession and the recession's inevitable effects on its profits and the value of its shares. A longer view over the past half-century reveals a much more hopeful and reassuring picture: an increasing willingness not only to respond to the forces of change but to influence the course of that change. From ranking somewhere in the lower part of the glass manufacturers' first league, it has now become a, if not *the*, world leader in the industry.

Index

(Numbers in italics refer to illustrations and diagrams)